THE EARTH REMEMBERS EVERYTHING

Caitlin Press Inc.
8100 Alderwood Road,
Halfmoon Bay, BC V0N 1Y1
www.caitlin-press.com

Text and cover design by Vici Johnstone.

"Mosquito Lake" (pg 11) was previously published by Contemporary
Verse 2: The Open Issue, Fall 2011.
"Chinlac in Dene means 'wood floats to'" was previously published by sub-
Terrain: Prince George Folio. Winter 2011.

Printed in Canada

Caitlin Press Inc. acknowledges financial support from the Government
of Canada through the Canada Book Fund and the Canada Council for
the Arts, and from the Province of British Columbia through the British
Columbia Arts Council and the Book Publisher's Tax Credit.

Canada Council Conseil des Arts   BRITISH COLUMBIA
for the Arts   du Canada   ARTS COUNCIL
                                   An agency of the Province of British Columbia

Library and Archives Canada Cataloguing in Publication

Fitzpatrick, Adrienne, 1966-

The earth remembers everything / Adrienne Fitzpatrick.

ISBN 978-1-894759-90-8

1. Atrocities. 2. Massacres. 3. World history.

4. Fitzpatrick, Adrienne, 1966- —Travel. I. Title.

D24.F58 2012   909   C2012-903360-X

The Earth
Remembers Everything

Adrienne Fitzpatrick

Caitlin Press

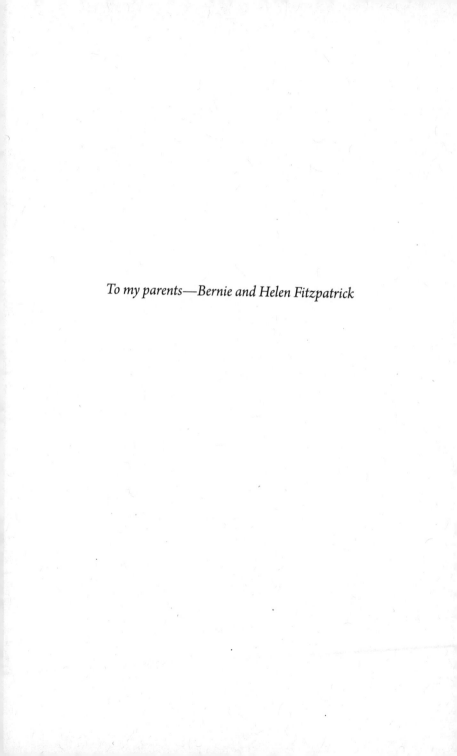

To my parents—Bernie and Helen Fitzpatrick

Contents

PREFACE

Place is prior to all things.
—Aristotle

To follow Aristotle's view, *The Earth Remembers Everything* is a phenomenological experience of place that transcends boundaries and barriers, whether they are personal, cultural or political. I believe that the profound is possible, and because of this, changes in perception, views and emotions surrounding experience of place are possible as well. This book is based on my own experience, with the intention to seek connections, to show how we are all implicated, indeed involved, in the subtle, sometimes shocking but always changing experience of place.

I acknowledge that it has been a great privilege to travel and to write about these places, and that my work engages in historical complexity, including colonialism, capitalism, racism, and appropriation issues. I could not tell my story without encroaching on these areas and I trust that the deep respect and compassion I felt at all of these massacre sites comes through in my work. I recognize that there are other views and stories of these places that have deep significance, not only personally, but to families, communities and entire cultures. The underlying theme of *The Earth Remembers Everything* is to express essence, not only of the experience of place, but of the self in place. Nothing can erase the past or the wounds incurred by it, but it is my hope that a profound sense of place can make room for connection and healing.

I chose excerpts from A.G. Morice's *The History of the Central Interior of British Columbia* as a basis for my fiction, with the view that his stories and accounts are also a somewhat fictionalized history of the area. The stories in *The History of the Central Interior of British Columbia* were translated from Carrier and Chilcotin into 19th Century English by Father Morice, who was a French Oblate priest with his own views on the area and its people. My intention was to weave the stories of the Carrier, which are powerfully rooted in place and to each other, with the stories of the places I travelled to and the people I travelled with. In my view, the memories and deep emotion the earth holds is the same as what exists within all of us. My hope is that these stories link not just the earth and its people, but show that what happened in the Central Interior of British Columbia a very long time ago is happening still on all corners of the earth.

This book is a blend of fiction and creative non-fiction, and it can also be seen as a personal travelogue. Though I went to these sites as a tourist, my intention was not to appropriate in any way a story that was not mine to tell. I wanted to be open to the experience. In my view, that is the responsibility of a traveller—to learn something about a culture as well as oneself. This is the attitude in which I approached this book. My interest in massacre sites is not only as sites of trauma but places of historical significance, where I could be affected by an experience larger than myself, and to possibly be opened up, changed and then able to learn more about my presence in the world.

Mosquito Lake

At the mushroom pickers' camp on Haida Gwaii there are stories of hauntings at nearby Mile 13 and Mosquito Lake. Legends of ghosts, mass killings, a wandering dead logger and a beast that stalks you in the woods.

Pickers came but they didn't stay, though it was beautiful. Mountains tusked with snow, clear deep lake. One or two nights and the dream would come.

"I don't believe it," says Nigel, the crooked-nosed Australian.

"I haven't had nightmares since I was a kid and my grandmother was standing at the foot of my bed," I say. "She had her dark heart in her hands. Her eyes were black holes."

"You dream of death at the lake." Toby, the blond skater, swigs back a beer. We are standing around a licking fire and the guts of berry-fed deer. "Lucy and I stayed there and we dreamed of marauders three nights in a row. You can see their faces, even your reflection in their eyes. Some heard drums, thump of running feet, cries of fear and war. Lucy woke up screaming, we packed up, slept in the truck on some logging road."

Dogs rummage through scraps, strips of dead deer. There are hunters and you know them. Your mother kills your father. Your sister has a gash on her arm, you can see bone. It won't heal. It won't heal. People you loved with your whole self. It was a massacre. The earth remembers everything.

POLAND

Leaning out the window of the train, hot spring sun warms my face, wind tears my eyes. Land slopes and rolls along, brilliant yellow fields, a few bored dogs watching. Rolling green hills with cottages needing an extra coat of paint; doors hanging off hinges, hammers, rusted saws strewn around. Fresh laundry needing to be gathered in from the yard. Passengers around us murmur and the rustle of dinner being unpacked prompts a "You hungry?" from Kat. Kat is short for Katherine. Tall, blonde and from Denver, she laughs easily, gives in to my whims. She's recovering from a failed affair. I was so distraught, I cried all the way to the airport, she said, slight grimace. Her ex had to pull over so she could gather herself, fake a bold front until it worked. In Prague, she is what my friends call a *flatmate*.

Our flat has round, wide windows and two balconies where we sit and smoke. We are teaching English to very smart, unimpressed students. I am stunned by their smooth beauty, showing up my peasant roots. They speak German, Russian and excellent English, laugh at my attempts to entertain. Gone are the days when every foreign teacher was a star. Slowly I make friends with Jiri and Jana. We go to absinthe bars, talk about the sweet smell of oranges that they had to line up for during Communist times. How the taste told them of other worlds. They laughed when I told them I didn't like castles, moats with chained bears, dark corridors with the heads of slain animals mounted.

"I am *starved*," I declare.

We have not even thought about making dinner so we go to the dining car, square tables with pale peach covers, fake carnations in white vases. Air smells of burnt butter, onions and the salty yeast of rising bread. We order goulash and dumplings from a sour-faced waiter.

With full stomachs and a glass of wine, we dodge stockinged and bare feet jutting out at odd angles in the aisle. Our beds have been made in our absence, a sleepy calm has descended. Soft sleeping sighs, eruption of snores. We flip coins and Kat gets the top bunk and we settle in for the night after a furtive trip to the bathroom to brush our teeth. Close the window, close the blinds, chat ourselves to sleep. What seems like minutes later we are shocked awake by the customs official standing at the entrance of our car. Bright hall lights illuminate the outline of his frame, short, bulky. His face is shaded by the wide brim of his cap. Businesslike voice requesting passports. He peruses our documents and hands them back, abruptly turns. Kat's voice booms:

"Can we get a stamp?"

"No," he grunts, annoyed, and is gone.

"No? Why not?" She trails off. "What a rude bastard," she whispers to me. We laugh a bit and the train rumbles and jerks. My body rolls to the sudden bursts of movement and I imagine all the other bodies on the train rolling, sleeping, rolling, sleeping.

That night I dream of our street in Prague, where I am sitting on our balcony that overlooks a narrow cobblestoned street. I am watching dream people walking below, no one I recognize. Then a tall thin man with a brown dog leaping and barking beside him turns the corner and walks up just below the balcony and stops. He is trying to control the dog but then it starts howling, long mournful sobs. They are both dishevelled, and I can't make out his face, just his mouth as he turns his head up to the sky, his lips move and a voice comes into my head *You must get ready*. Such a clear, urgent voice. I wake up immediately. Kat's hand dangles near the window.

We arrive at 7:00 a.m., grab some bread and sausage at the station and find a cab to take us to our hostel. The driver, distracted, balding, barely looks at us when we get in and we are already moving when he glances at our address, nods. Our hostel turns out to be a college dormitory with a long stall of showers. From across the courtyard we can see men showering, steam clouds, glints of skin.

～

Krakow is cobblestoned, smooth brick buildings, winking windows, nuns in dark robes flit across side streets, imposing churches on every block. We trudge the slow incline of a road to the church where Pope John Paul preached, passing tourists with cameras, stores with fresh irises in the windows. At the church, which is somehow quiet though crammed with people, there is a bell the size of a small house at the top of a narrow winding stair. I imagine it rings with a depth and clarity that I have never heard.

"Stop crying!" A stylish middle-aged mother hisses at her daughter.

The child is pale, blotchy and sniffling, with long, dark braided hair and pink shoes. "I'm tired!"

Mother and daughter are at a standoff on the stairs.

"Travel is hell," Kat whispers under her breath.

After the church we scramble down an embankment to the river. "What's the river called?" I ask Kat but I know she doesn't know. We travel well together. No forced conversation. Instant intimacy that often comes with travelling, family histories, past loves, has sparked fast friendship. Hurts bask in the open air of our balcony, seem less daunting. The word *regroup* comes up, and *space*. I listen to Kat, glass of wine in hand, passing a smoke. I don't want to be home, I tell her. Japan changed me, the world opened up. I was going to Kyoto every weekend, climbing mountains to the tiny temples and listening to cicadas, bamboo click clack in the wind, watching monkeys scurry up the paths, careful not to look them in the eye to avoid a possible attack. I want to keep going, feel constrained so easily, and I am lucky and selfish right now, discontented, restless and unwilling at this moment to grab what is lying there, just below the surface, shimmering and alive.

"What does it look like," she asks, "this shimmering?"

"An exotic fish, a koi in a Chinese garden, a salmon, bucking free in the ocean. Do you know that a salmon molts, that it loses its skin like a snake when it returns home?"

We lean back in our chairs, into the world like it will hold us so we can do some great thing, or escape for a little while, or heal. Krakow continues on the other side of the river and for as far as we can see. Warm June sun melts us into a lounging recline on the concrete ledge where we perch.

DENE

The Carrier village of Chinlac is on the far side of Stuart Lake and is best reached by canoe in the summer months. When I was in high school, there were class trips to Chinlac, as it was and is an archaeological site, a place of artifacts, of memory. There were photographs in the school yearbook of campsites and clowning students and I heard stories of haunting, shadowy presences, sleepless nights. There was a massacre at this site in 1745 but I had a dim idea of what *massacre* meant. Certainly something bloody and raw, occurring for reasons unknowable and primal. This was my teenage version of things. A Catholic priest, Father Morice, spent ten years in Fort St. James and worked closely with the Carrier. Previously, he had lived in Williams Lake and began his study of Chilcotin as well as Carrier, and became proficient in both languages. He learned and transcribed their stories.

The main tribes of the Northern Interior are divided into four. The Sekanais occupy the western slope of the Rocky Mountains and all the adjoining territory, reaching as far as the 53rd latitude. The Babines inhabit the shores of the lake called after them and the Bulkley Valley, though many of them hunt near French and Cambie lakes. The Carriers have villages all the way from Stuart Lake to Alexandria on the Fraser, and the Chilcotins mainly occupy the valley of the river to which they have given their name.

These tribes form the Western Denes. *Dene* means men.

POLAND

A white, dusty bus picks us up at 7:30 a.m. and we are the first ones in, so we take the best seats near the front. The driver is long and skinny, carrying on an intense conversation with the portly, middle-aged tour guide. It is all in Polish but Kat and I play a game and pretend that they're discussing their uptight boss, stupid tourists, money, a really good restaurant. Pros and cons of buying a country home. Conversations that would be irritating, funny or intriguing, if we could understand them, but in another language, they're like a spell being cast. Words parsed, mysterious, incantatory like chanting of the Buddhist monks in Japan, in Thailand, in Laos, the *om* that thrums and buzzes, burrows into you and then bursts out. *Om.* On the labyrinthine journey to pick up the others at their hotels, the city is just waking up. Warm spring air drifts and huddles in the corners of tiny cafés; we pass bakeries where customers stand catatonic, their morning mouths churning bread and coffee like cud, gruel of life. Finally the bus is full and our tour guide introduces himself as Josef, born and raised in Krakow. His voice is slow, sombre and matches the solemn blue of his eyes. The other tourists are middle-aged and formally dressed, khaki shorts, crisp white shirts and blouses. Sensible walking shoes.

He stands in front of the bus and starts talking, his

slow, deep voice rising just above the rustling and mumbling. He knows eventually people will stop talking and listen; he has done this a million times, his eyes blanking out our faces. "The drive to Auschwitz will take an hour and a half. There is a short film at the museum and then you are free to wander the camp and take in its exhibits. There are guided tours in a variety of languages if you wish. After a few hours there, we will regroup and go to Birkenau for a few hours in the afternoon. There are guided tours there as well." Josef counts our nodding heads. "There are twelve of you. Don't get lost. We leave Birkenau at three and will be back in Krakow for dinner, drop you off at your hotels." He sits down and resumes his involved conversation with the driver.

City melts away and the country homes are tidy, all the laundry and tools gathered in, folded and packed away. Everything in its place. Window shutters painted in smart shades of red, lawns are cut and flowers toss their luscious June yellow, pink and purple coifs. Kat nods off in the seat beside me, sun lighting half her face, her firm brown arms. A couple behind us share a muffin, slurp coffee, mumble "where's the guide book, how far did he say it was?" Heads are nodding, rolling side to side. Did they have relatives that died here? My ancestors could have died here. They could have been the killers.

I need to see the wound.

There's a bubble of silence that happens when the home of language is not available, a reprieve from the constant change and decision-making, tinged with loneliness. It is not unlike waiting in line at the bank or a store, a kind of enforced meditation. Homesickness strikes, a sucker punch, then ebbs. In an hour we arrive and tumble out of the bus; we join a crowd of hundreds, it seems, filing into a large building where the movie will be shown. Wooden chairs shuffle and scrape the cement floor in a large, cool, utilitarian room and the movie is old, black and white with trains and children and it flies by me. I don't catch a word. I don't get it at all. Lights go on and the exit doors open and we are turned out into the sun like children at recess and there it is. *Arbeit Macht Frei.*

This sign like some omen shivers me when I pass under it, crossing over into ghost town brick buildings with curved roofs separated by dirt footpaths, patches of flourishing grass. Glassed-in rooms separated by the creak of knotted wooden floors, piles of hair, piles of glasses, piles of clothes, piles of toys. Crutches, plastic legs, plastic arms. Piles of shoes, kid-sized, women's heels. Small dark rooms with slatted spaces for air where people spent days in solitary. In an empty courtyard there is a pole with a hook on it. I hear one of the tour guides say that this was where people were punished; they were hung howling by their wrists for hours.

"Do you want to get a tour guide?" Kat whispers, like we are being watched.

"I don't know. How much do you want to know?"

She looks at me, squinting in the sun. Groups are thronging through the camp, huddled close to their guides like clinging children. We stand in the middle of the road for a few moments.

"What do you think of all the mounds of stuff?"

25

I ask Kat. "Is that what becomes of us? A pair of glasses?"

"Maybe," she says. "It's hot. Your chest is turning red. Did you bring a shirt?"

"Yeah." I pull a blue cotton long sleeve out and shuck it on. It clings to my clammy skin.

We follow the crowds to a small building with a flat roof, a half-buried bunker. People are lining up to get in and there is a steady stream coming out, uniform marching ants. As we get closer a couple of young women dressed in shorts and tanks ahead of us stop suddenly, hands on hips.

"I'm *not* going in there!" One of them cries out as Kat and I approach.

"What is it?" I ask. They are both blonde, a bit plump, strong Australian accents.

"It's the ovens," the one closest to me says, distraught.

"Where you from?"

"Melbourne," they both answer.

We stand and chat a bit about Krakow. They are staying close to our hostel and introduce themselves as Lila and Linda. Sisters.

"This place is horrible," Linda laughs, rueful. "We're heading back to the bus."

"I don't know why we came here," Lila says, and they turn around.

"Should we?" I'm curious, feel dirty. "Let's go." We follow the crowd, line up like pilgrims to see something holy. Descending the three steps, an oppressive wave of heat shot through with sweat hits, room is cramped, guides talk above the shuffling and mumbling. "This was the first gas chamber at the camp and it was kept to show the annihilation that was going on here…" The largest chambers and ovens were at Birkenau but they have been destroyed. What happened was this: the inmates were segregated into two groups, women and children together and then the men. They were told they were going to bathe so everyone took off their clothes. Once they entered the chambers, gas came out of the walls. There was no water. Panic soaked in, changed molecules of steel and cement like a force field, toxic, undiluted. Small bits like shrapnel absorb into our bodies, like gas seeping in, silent flood. Ledges of seats and little shower heads like the stalls at our hostel, innocent, utilitarian.

For a moment we are submerged, buried alive in consuming tongues of panic, arms and legs pounding in fear and then futility against the steel walls. Like a drum still percussing, reverberating fear, flowing out in waves, a grenade exploding the sea. We emerge from the chamber disoriented, stand in the sun. Breathe. It is time to head back to the bus.

Faces of the other travellers are flushed, overwhelmed. I am reminded of another hot bus full of tourists in Chiang Mai, where shooting rapids in a bamboo raft and hiking in the hills to Hmong villages created a casual camaraderie that connected us. Here, we are confronted by enormity, by horror and history and it is too much to talk about. Eyes are averted. Quiet reigns, thoughts reined in. Sombre Josef announces we will be at Birkenau in fifteen minutes.

✑

Brzezinka. Polish word for birch

Auschwitz has three simple words to introduce its horror. Birkenau has train tracks and a narrow brick train station, relentless stare of the lookout tower. Kat and I find a map of the site at the tourist centre and start our exploration through the rows of barracks, blank buildings, dirt floors. Deep, battered sinks for washing. Wooden slats of bunks in stacks of three. Grounds feel like a graveyard. Barracks are memorials with no written names, fringed with stark, thin birch trees, sky wide and void of birds singing, flying.

"Here is the place where the old women were left to starve," Kat points at a mark on the map, crumpled and sweaty in her wide hands.

When the women became too old or ill to work anymore, they were moved here and given no food or water. Warm wind blows through the hollow centre, shafts of dirt fan the doorways and on to the next one, where a painting hangs of German officials in dark blue, thick severe moustaches still menacing. They are holding clubs in their hands, waving them in the air. *Konigsburg* is written above the scene.

The earth has absorbed so much emotion that all it has the energy to do is grow grass. It is June and the buildings are dappled. I would love a smoke but I won't, it would feel like a desecration. All the crematoriums have been destroyed. Flat pieces of concrete mark where they were and memorials of bright yellow daffodils, soft pink carnations, black and white photos rest on the corners of memory. Kat and I settle on one, concrete heat rough on our bare legs, passing a bottle of water between us. The unknowable hovers at the entrances, the gates, the railroad, rises up through the soles of my feet. We walk back to the bus, weary, like we are wading through knee-deep water instead of grass. Ride back is quiet, even Josef and the driver have worn out their conversation. Something has been settled, maybe, between them, the world fitting back in to where it should be, and we are the voyeurs of black holes. The earth remembers everything.

DENE

Na'kwoel is the first really historical aborigine mentioned by the Carrier Indians of Stuart Lake. Agreement is that his birthdate is 1660 and his name became the symbol of old age. He was short and very corpulent, which was quite rare among the Western Denes. He held the position of *toeneza,* or hereditary nobleman, of the Stuart Lake clan and was the first Dene to own an iron axe or adze, which he acquired in 1730 from the village of Tsechah, which is now Hazelton, on the Skeena. He held a great feast for his fellow tribesmen and the adze hung like swinging gold from the rafters of the lodge to be admired. Na'kwoel kept it always within his sight except one winter, when it fell off a bough it was tied to into the snow. It was found only after a Medicine Man divined it, being led by the spirits through his prayers.

One day when Na'kwoel was butchering a caribou on solid lake ice, killed and brought to him by friendly neighbours, he heard footsteps on the frozen snow. Bold, they echoed in the stillness, then a sudden stop. It was a native of Natleh, Fraser Lake, and Na'kwoel immediately seized his bow and arrow and aimed it at the unwelcome intruder.

"You know that we do not speak with people from Natleh. Why are you here?"

The visitor pretended not to notice and if he was

afraid, he hid it well. Snow blew veils of white dust between them. He looked straight into Na'kwoel's eyes and walked over to where other members of Na'kwoel's tribe stood on the lake, watching. They welcomed the stranger and talked and laughed for some time when the stranger suddenly bent his bow and aimed his arrow at Na'kwoel.

"Who are you, old Na'kwoel, who will not speak to our people? What reason do I have not to sink this arrow between your ribs?"

The men stood on the firm ice in taut silence, waiting for some word or gesture of forgiveness or aggression. Na'kwoel's sharp dark eyes took their time deciding and eventually his body bent back to his work. The stranger from Natleh chatted and laughed awhile longer and then returned to his village, named for the salmon that come back.

POLAND

On our last day in Krakow, we come across the Remuh synagogue beside the Jewish cemetery, a smooth, white-washed building guarded by a black gate, and up winding stairs there is a gathering of school-age children surrounding an old man, short, bald, sagging blue eyes with a bit of dance in them. Laughing, he clears his throat, and a quiet descends. The kids are expectant. American, we find out from a translator, a bright-eyed woman with a bouncy dark ponytail.

"The man is a Holocaust survivor, one of Oskar Schindler's kids," she says by way of introduction. "He was chosen from the Krakow ghetto at the age of ten and worked in one of Schindler's factories making mess kits for the German soldiers."

"I was very scared." His voice muffled, a bit shy. "But I kept quiet, kept busy, for my family. Most of whom, including my mother, father and brother, were killed at Auschwitz." Placid face, no wrinkle of emotion worries it.

"I survived the war by working in factories and by the time it was over I was a young man and an apprentice mechanic. I never left Krakow." I notice that a few teeth are missing in his warm smile. "And when I turned twenty-one, I married a Catholic girl and we had five children!" He laughs to himself and the talk ends. Everyone claps enthusiastically.

That night at the hostel we watch the men shower from the women's bathroom. They preen, soap up, some shave, shampoo rolling down their faces in white waves. "They know we are watching," I tell Kat. They are putting on a show. We eat bread and cheese in our room and then go out to the town square, drink wine while the gypsies make their rounds, playing violins, a tattered guitar. They are young.

"Ten? Eleven?" I say to Kat.

Some part of me is hollowed out, a clear space for the wind to blow through. We almost miss our train even though we've had all day to get ready, we scramble and swear on the platform. *God.* What is wrong with us?

Later we laugh, roll and rock in our narrow beds like babies. We return to Prague and discover that our other flatmate, Robert, has left without paying rent. No note, just dust under his vacated bed. I see this as a sign and I decide to go home. It is the summer of 2004. Kat stays on, finds a job, falls in and out of love with a Czech man and moves to England. I find a job in Vancouver and begin the process of what I call normal life, but I'm restless. Kat meets a man in the army and begins a long-distance relationship. She moves back to Colorado and teaches but is restless too.

What is it? she writes to me. *This urge.*

In 2008, I go to Ho Chi Minh City to work for a friend for six months, which extends to a year because I fall in love with a Japanese man. I am becoming unhappy though I try to convince myself I am fine. Kat finds a job travelling with a retired army captain who wants to go back to Vietnam before he dies. She makes the arrangements, keeps him company. When they come to Ho Chi Minh City, I meet Kat at a Lebanese restaurant down one of the narrow, twisting dark alleys. There is outdoor seating, plush pillows, candles, puffs of sweet apple hookah smoke. When I see her I begin to sing, *and the Kat came back, the very next day, yes, the Kat came back, we thought she was a goner, but the Kat came back the very next day, the Kat couldn't stay away.* She is effusive, laughing, tanned, wearing big silver hoops and heels that show off her shapely, athletic legs.

"Should I leave him?" she asks me. "I never see him."

"I don't know. Do you love him?"

"Love is the least of it." She sips her wine. "I can't stay here. It kills me to leave him but this is not for me."

We order tangines and a bottle of wine. It has been four years since our trip to Krakow, since we lived in our flat with the balcony where we talked, smoked, healed a little. We don't mention Auschwitz or Birkenau but it is still there, all the neat rows and piles. Hook gouged into a post for hanging.

Mosquito Lake

Toby dreams he crosses the lake. Marauders throw flaming hatchets past his head, hiss as they plunge. He paddles an old canoe, insides scooped out, scratched raw. He can hear the howl follow, searing sound. Leaves of skin glint in sinking waves, glow of bone. Water still cold after all that burning. Canoe reaches a hill so steep he scuttles sideways. Shell of torn jacket pummelled with cones, branches tired of holding. All this dreaming war, arrows slice. Salal rustles, grumbling bear gnawing roots, berries. Blood pounding shifting guts speckled sweat. As a child he made shadows on grass, the shape of a cross. He did not dream then. Bear becomes his father, smooth hair glowing skin. Only circle of light in the forest. When Toby wakes, Lucy is screaming.

Who knows how the war started. A word, a look, a killing. Blades and arrows thrown till they thud, wrenched out, thrown again. Such horror doesn't dull, wakes up when the earth slumbers. A killing, a word, a look, and it begins again.

Mile 13

Toby and Nigel refuse to go to Mile 13 to pick mush-
rooms. No one will go except Cook. Efficient, he chops,
cuts, carries. Chanterelles he picks show up in omelettes,
in stews, peppery and light.

"There must be more where they came from," Corey
says. "Picking territory gets snatched up quickly. Here's
a chance to grab ours."

"But isn't it Cook's territory?" I say, judicious, try-
ing to back out for good reason. Respecting tribal lines,
invisible to me but inscribed as surely as any drawn on
a map.

"He doesn't care, I asked him." Corey gives me a
level gaze. So it is decided. We're going in. We're going in
with buckets that used to hold oil, cleaned out, scoured
but with a whiff of noxious residue. Bear bells, fluores-
cent rain gear that is not standing up to the weather. Box
cutters as mushroom scalpels. Packs around our waists
with nuts, raisins, chocolate chips. Gardening gloves for
a firm grip of the thin plastic handle. My fingers ache in
them. Dirt still clings to my scalp after my shower yes-
terday, imprint of permanent earth on my knees. Corey
insists that we bring bright pink tape to mark our way in
so we can find our way out.

"But we have a compass," I say. They don't always
work here, he tells me. Something about iron deposits

or the ghost of a logger killed here awhile back, sliced up at the green chain, messes with the directions. The green chain, a makeshift mill with a giant saw, is at the centre of a clearing, Corey tells me, a few miles north from the road. I imagine a crude gallows, where trees refuse to grow, moss shrivels from branches. Impatient to get going, he is already climbing the embankment, looking over his shoulder: "Come on!"

An experienced picker, Corey offers terse instructions. Make sure you wear cork boots, double tie your laces. Stop to take a reading on your compass at the top of a hill, every few hundred feet if you can remember. Watch where you step, it's easy to break an ankle if you slip between logs. I am careful, careful like I am carrying tea cups in my hands while walking tightrope. Moisture coats my face, twists my hair into a thick, unmovable wave. At night we are so exhausted we hardly speak and in the morning I wake up first, make coffee in the blue-tarp lean-to, sit on the cold bench. Mist makes pools in the hollows of the road. Knees, elbows ache. No-see-ums, tiny transparent flies, dive into my eyes, ears, try to crawl up my nose. Bites and unbearable itch force me down the road, involuntary morning walk.

We met in a bar in Vancouver, long glances over brims of beer. On a break from tree planting contracts, he told me about Haida Gwaii, about Yoho, sand dunes in Oregon. Letters with pressed purple, orange, blue petals, seeds settled at the crease of the envelope. Smell of stony mountain slopes, sun-warmed earth. Three months later we are squatting on an abandoned logging road, huddling together for warmth, instructions filling the up and down of our days. Passing patches of trees ripped and strewn and rotting. Every so often I stop to tie ribbons on sturdy branches, so they will stand out from the blobs of moss, bulbous mounds thick at the base of trees, spatters from a child's paint brush.

Corey tells me about the time he was lost for days in the forest, kept alive with berries and water from streams. He was so cold and thirsty that it consumed his fear. Panicked, he wandered at first and then he gave in, surrendered out of exhaustion. Helicopters and other pickers searched the hillsides of the territory where he picked, guessing that he had hit a patch of iron ore, metal that disturbed his compass. He was found huddled at the base of a tree and cried with relief, shaky when he walked out. A rookie, he was bolder, less afraid, he said, more aware than before he got lost. He went picking after a few days' rest and stopped talking about it altogether. There isn't a lot to say when you are alone in the woods. When you know where you're going and the picking is good, the forest is friendly. When you are cold and lost, the moss turns into shrouds, keeping you from the light. You fold in, focus on survival, on imminent rescue. Like after a meal when all the blood rushes to your stomach, all your thoughts crowd around that one thing.

"Does the ghost do anything?" I ask. Our feet make hollow sounds on the moss like we are treading softly on the moon. Smell of earth beneath, taste of sea. I am hungry but it is too soon for lunch.

"No. He watches," Corey answers, out of breath

from a fight through a salal bush. Streaks of blood from scratches graze his fair skin, leaves stick out of his hair, sheaves of wheat ruffling his collar.

Trailing blobs of bright pink ribbon, we continue north. I think of the van, peaceful behind us, long to be safe in the seat, rolling down the road. In the gully below, a patch of peach chanterelles calls out to Corey, who descends on them, ravenous gatherer. I catch my breath, cold sweat slips down my spine. While he can spot them instantly, it takes a few minutes for them to peep out at me from the moss and rot where they hide. Clamber over fallen logs, haul our half-full pails over and crouch down to cut. Monotony of trees, trying to calm my sea-sick stomach. Constant fear of bears. At the campfire in the evening there are stories, bears eating salal berries surprised by a sudden face in the bush. Curious ones climb trees, claws ripping through thin bark.

"You're supposed to make noise, fight fear, jump up and down," says Lucy, and the pickers nod.

"We are a bony nuisance or novelty," Corey says. Fire licks the dried wood and roasting deer, raw meat browning.

As I lean down and cut, heat blazes the back of my neck, unmistakable sense of presence. Corey cuts stems and doesn't raise his head, so I carry on. Stories pass the barriers of knowing. I could be making it up. Down the next hill, our buckets covered with old t-shirts to keep the leaves and moss out.

"Let's stop for lunch," I say to the back of his head.

"We've just started," he looks at me, frustrated.

"Do you feel like someone is watching you?" He looks at me blankly; no, he doesn't. "Why? Do you?"

"Yeah, when we were picking I thought someone was staring at me. Felt like *get out*, you know?"

"Yeah, well, there's plenty of good picking. The ghost isn't going to hurt you."

DENE

Na'kwoel had two sons, A'ke'toes and Chichanit, both of whom wielded great influence among their fellow tribesmen, with A'ke'toes in line to become hereditary chief. He was a fierce, jealous man whose demons forced his two wives, Chalh'tas and Atete, to live in isolated seclusion, fighting off accusations of unfaithfulness. Tormented and lonely, Chalh'tas was quick to anger and fought often with her husband. Atete was more submissive, overwhelmed by the demands of her husband and Chalh'tas. A'ke'toes was believed to have the forces of evil at his command, to be possessed by malicious spirits that could prove fatal to himself and those close to him. He was feared by the Carrier and was protected by the love of Na'kwoel.

One such secluded place where the family stayed was Long Island, at the outlet of Stuart Lake, five miles from the village of Tsauche, where their tribesmen lived on the same lake. A violent fight started between A'ke'toes and Chalh'tas, in which she accused him of the recent death of her two children. It started like many of their fights, angry words hurled like stones, raining down wounds, but this day it escalated to a raging storm of blows and Chalh'tas became determined to kill her husband. She fell on him and cried out to Atete to help her.

"If you do not help me I will kill you myself!" she

screamed at Atete, who fell on A'ke'toes with more fear than rage. They beat him to death and dismembered his remains, Chalh'tas triumphant; Atete swallowed her shame. They carried his bones to the mouth of a stream emptying on the opposite side of the lake, and buried them in the sand.

MILE 13

Cook heard about Mile 13 from the loggers at the boarding house breakfast table years ago, men twisted over eggs and porridge, knotted and rough. No one had been there in awhile, green chain blade was slimy with moss but there were plenty of trees to be taken, that's for sure. Wouldn't recommend going alone, son, they said.

"I'd just moved from the mainland. Didn't know anyone," Cook said. We are in the cooking shack, chopping vegetables for venison stew. I help him out, rest from the bush. And it's warm in the shack, out of the rain.

"They told me 'it's a two-man job, and with you, maybe three.'" They laughed at him, chortling around the table. He decided then to go, report back to the geezers that Mile 13 was his. He had been shadowing for a week now, bucked a few trees on his own and it was time to stake his territory. No one would stop him at Mile 13.

"I was skinny then, not like now," he pats his soft stomach. He grew up in the Interior, the lakes and rivers and open space of the Carrier. Lithe, he slipped through the rainforest and wasn't stopped by the thick salal. Only homesick in the evenings, he told me, he would've written to his aunt but he didn't know how. He learned the basics in school, the loops and curves of his name but he quit in grade eight, didn't learn how to write his insides.

Packed lunch in his burlap sack, the truck let him off at Mile 13 to raised eyebrows and silence. Sack slung across his shoulder, he carried his chainsaw and axe up the embankment and into the soft moss. Quiet closed in, moist embrace. He stopped every once in awhile to rest, chainsaw weighing his right side. I can see him, picking his way through, sharp eyes measuring huge trees that crowded out the sun. Moss dripping from branches, sound of wings, *tchock, tchock, tchock* of a raven. Breath rising and falling with the hills. Last night, I dreamed the hills were swelling waves, rising higher and higher until I was crawling, hand to knee, like a child.

"It may have been going on for awhile but there was the sound of breathing." Sizzle of frying venison, air thick with herbs and oil, we both stir steadily. "It was heavy, like an animal dying right beside me. Reminded me of a horse my uncle shot that had been hit by a truck. And it tried so hard to keep breathing. Sounded like that. And the smell of shit was so strong, almost made me sick." He kept stirring, I added onions. "Felt like someone was watching me, you know? When your neck gets all hot, you look around and no one is there. *Frick.* Thought that maybe one of the men had followed to scare me, but there was no way that breathing was from a man."

"What did you do?" I asked. Cook wiped his hands on his smudged apron, lit a smoke, bits of white and black hair in his eyes.

"Thought I would scare it off, take a swing with my axe, make some noise. I yelled really loud, *aaaaaaaaahh-hhhhh*, maybe it was a bear. Started up my chainsaw and I bucked a tree, chunks were flying. Kind of like, this is my territory, leave me alone."

Shaking, sweating, too afraid to look anywhere but straight ahead to the next hill, he told me the smell got worse. Thing was breathing like its lungs were full, a slow drowning. Cook grabbed his gear, moved on. There was money in the woods, he wasn't going back until he saw the size of the trees. And he didn't want the men to know he was afraid.

At the top of the next hill, there was a clearing with a trail of mushrooms in a dip of valley below. By a shredding trunk was a pyramid of mussel shells, perfectly shaped, stacked in precise diagonals. Pile came to just past his knees when he got up close.

"Who could eat all that?" He looked at me, his eyes narrowed. "*Frick.* This was no place for a picnic, believe me." Breathing became a high-pitched scream like a warning, off to his right.

"It was beside me, close enough that there was a dark shadow in the bush. Screaming right at me, I could feel its eyes." Rasping gasps curdled breath. He knew then the horror behind the silence of the men and he hated them, he told me, angrily hacking up the venison for the second pot of stew.

"I couldn't go back, it kept walking beside me. It didn't get any closer but it didn't go. *Frick.* I made it to the green chain, notched a few more trees, show it that it was my territory now, it had better go." Cook swept his arm in front of him, clearing an invisible path.

Mosquito Lake

Toby got lost past Mosquito Lake last night. Said all night he was so thirsty, he was more thirsty than afraid. And here there is so much water. I'd be so hungry I'd see fish frying in the bush, smell the smoke if I let myself. Or remember things like when my best friend left in grade nine I wrote a poem about her by the side of a choppy lake. Maybe I'd remember that. I think maybe I would remember lying down in the sand in some hot place, feeling the completeness of my body, stretched, supple. What does it matter when it's dark and there's no one to listen. Keeping your flashlight on till it burns out. You're in some war movie you watched when you were a kid and safe on the couch. Keeping your wits about you as though someone would steal them. Laugh while they're taking them.

Mile 13

Horror of the sound passed like the shock of pain after a blow. Cook stopped wondering what it was. He could still hear the heavy thump of footsteps beside him, keeping pace. Dense like a moving mountain, whatever it was, pungent smell warning him to stay on edge.

We are taking a break, sharing a smoke by Skidegate Lake, grey and motionless, sprouting stalky reeds like spears.

Outline of the green chain in the bush reminded him of an extinct animal. "Some kind of long, lean raptor with a gouged crown down its back," he said, his face drawn, his compact body sprawled on a log. "There were piles of logs waiting to be cut, so I turned on the generator, found the switch for the blade and it was a little wobbly, but it worked." Eyes watched him but he ignored it. Maybe it would run at the screech of the blade, sound of money rolling in.

"Then a huge beast comes into the clearing, dark matted hair. Tiny black eyes, teeth bared, a wide squashed nose. Smell so strong I could hardly breathe." Cook stood up on the log, his short thick arms flung straight up beside his head, trying to convey its size, but I can't picture it. "We stood and looked at each other. It was breathing like it was dying but I couldn't see the wound."

After lunch, we continue to the green chain. Corey hasn't seen it in years and he wants to show me the scene of the crime. Back of my neck is still tingling, burn of eyes, but I try to put it out of my mind. It's just a story. Logger was killed so long ago there can't be anything left of him here. Further in we go, the more nervous I get. It's always like this, like wading into the ocean past your head until you're walking underwater. Further and further away from the van and the road, where the clear light hits and you can see the next bend, comforting curve. I stand at the next hill and check my compass. Due north it points and Corey is already heading down to the next mushroom patch. His internal radar is alert, he doesn't need the safety of checking and re-checking.

"This is it. Our new territory. We have to come at least once a week, these buttons need to grow some more, waste to pick them now." He glances over his shoulder at me with a look of *are you listening?* He sees me staring at the next hill, bright pink ribbon tied to the end of a mossy branch. I have tied well and carefully and it is easy to see from here. I point to it, say, there's a ribbon I tied and we're going north, I just checked.

Corey says nothing, leaves his buckets where the mushrooms are and hikes up the hill, grabs the branch, checks it and keeps going straight down the next hollow, up the next mossy hill. Checking the ribbons on the branches to be sure that we have come full circle in the maze, that we are being led out the way we came in.

VIETNAM

Vietnam is oppressive wet heat, apocalyptic murk hangs in the air, ground particles, detritus from the war that everyone breathes in, though no one ever talks about it. Relentless roar of sputtery motorcycles swerving and swaying on pocked streets, skimming by pedestrians, guided by road warriors, expressionless eyes, faces covered with cloth masks that look surgical from a distance but when I buy my own, they are pink and blue, patterned with flowers, ribbons. Long black ponytails and high heels mark out the women. Men wear cheap flip-flops and sag a bit more in their seats. Terror slows my steps so that it takes me half an hour to cross an intersection.

"Act like you're a pylon," Winnie says, "and they will go around you." Winnie is my friend and my boss, giving me the benefit of her time and experience, showing me where to shop, what restaurants are good, how much you can expect to pay for clothes and food.

"Which cabs are the good ones?"

"The white ones with the green writing. Drivers speak some English usually and they won't rip you off." She has lived in Saigon for five years already and is adept, matter of fact. I rent a room in the centre of the city in a narrow cinder-block building, blue tile with white skinny balconies, Lego'd amongst yellow, pink, green blocks, pushing up against the pavement, the confines of narrow alleys, looking for space to grow.

Within a week I am working and I have a *xe om*, motorcycle driver, Mr. Quang, who picks me up at my door for work. He must be in his fifties and so slight that I have to be careful not to crowd him off his seat. A makeshift café with plastic stools sets up every morning in the alley, along with the fruit lady and a couple that make sandwiches. The young husband has a cowlick, he is always smoothing it across his gleaming forehead. Coffee is thick and sweet, the bread crunchy with feathery insides, tang of pickle and salt of hot fried egg. Young men in dark blue pants and crisp white shirts smoke, laugh, ice tinkling on their teeth, constantly checking their cellphones. Sleek SUVs squeeze by, picking up expat executives, holding up the constant hum of motorcycles for a moment but then they veer around like ants encountering obstacles. Drivers stand and chat with the men drinking coffee and mothers half drag their uniformed children to school. Harry Potter backpacks, smiling Winnie the Pooh. At work, I am interviewing young Vietnamese for jobs with our clients, checking for English, confidence, good eye contact. Applicants, mainly young women, are eager and want to work for foreign, prestigious companies. Is the boss a foreigner? If not, they are not interested: No chance to improve English.

One lunch break, I find a new restaurant, a two-storey outdoor café with a pond on the main floor, flash of fins in murky water. From bins of food I pick out fried pork chops, rice and green beans, find a table on the top deck, wreathed with hanging lanterns, fringe of elegant trees. Leaves flicker in the breeze. Burn holes in the red tablecloths, glasses of iced beer click, laughter. It was difficult to walk here, crumbling sidewalks crowded with parked motorcycles, vendors selling t-shirts, coconuts, handbags from China. A charming waiter teaches me numbers, writing them out on my stained paper placemat.

"One is *mo*!" He declares in his laughing way. His hair is styled to stand straight up with the use of gel, which does not flag in the heat.

"*Mo, hai, ba*! That's one, two, three. It's also what you say for drinking. *Mot tram. Say mo jam*, means one hundred." He shows me a one-hundred dong note with the beatific face of Ho Chi Minh. I go to the outdoor café twice a week and eventually learn the numbers, which I cobble together with my street and the first thing I learn is my address—*moi tam bis wee tee minh kai*. I am triumphant. I can find my way home.

I go to the backpacker district, Pham Ngu Lao, to seek out company; busy blocks of hostels, restaurants, bars, internet cafés, revellers drinking beer, waves of tourists, of Vietnamese on the sidewalks, chatting in alleys. Indoor and outdoor markets crowd narrow streets, tables with raw lumps of beef, pork, squirming fish, bundles of bananas, coconuts, stern women calling children out of the street. One night I meet a woman from Vancouver, Teresa, middle-aged and chubby with a green and yellow scarf shot through with silver tied in her unruly hair, cheeks flushed from the beer and the heat. She was on her way home after two months living in Phnom Penh, volunteering at an international aid organization.

"I lived by the river and watched old people pick through the garbage every morning. The riverbank is full of hotels with old foreign men and young Cambodian girls they rent. It's disgusting. The heat, the bugs, my place was a dump… I kept trying to talk to the girls saying don't do it, they're pigs. But they need the money. It's awful. I didn't know what else to say. There was this great restaurant. I went there all the time. The owners were so wonderful." Putting down her glass, she looked at me with bewildered eyes. "I wondered what I was doing there. I felt so useless."

DENE

The women hid his bows and arrows in the woods and rocks of Stuart River and fled to Fraser Lake, leaving behind a message with the Tsauche tribe that following one of their usual disputes, A'ke'toes had tried to kill them but they escaped his wrath in his canoe. When he tried to pursue them he went past the level of his skill and drowned. Believing the story, the Stuart Lake tribe searched the river for days, where they recovered his missing quiver. A few days after this they recovered his mangled remains buried in the sand. The pain and anger Na'kwoel and Chichanit felt knew no bounds and they guarded this feeling, kept the need for revenge alive through the years after the wives disappeared.

Living in exile started to wear on Atete. She missed her family and wished to return home. Feeling vindicated by being the unwilling accomplice in the murder, she decided to end her exile and tell the whole truth of the matter to her tribe, hoping to have a happy homecoming. But as she neared Stuart Lake her return was revealed to Chichanit, whose rage sent him out to the edge of the lake and he killed her with his bow point—a spear fixed to the end of a bow—before she had a chance to speak. He later found out that Atete was coerced by Chalh'tas in the murder of A'ke'toes and he repented, feeling shame that she was unable to explain herself. He then decided to spare the life of guilty Chalh'tas if she became his wife in memory of his late brother. Messengers were sent back and forth and Chalh'tas agreed to the arrangement, which was quite common then. Widows often re-married their late husband's nearest kin.

Vietnam

When I pick my way around the hawkers and travellers to our appointed meeting spot, the *Sinh*, or Peace Café, Kelly is waiting, reading a travel guide, his Singha beer t-shirt already sticking to his bit of belly.

"Kelly!"

He rises. "*Adrienne*!" Big warm bear hug, he is clean-shaven, leaner than when he is at home. He is known, familiar, like a landmark.

"How was your trip?"

"Fine. Got in last night, ended up arguing with the cab driver, he was driving around in circles, running up the meter." We order bacon and eggs, Vietnamese coffee.

"How are you?" he asks, looking over at me quickly. DeTham Street in front of us is a crowd of taxis, buses, ladies in matching print tops and bottoms like pajamas, old bowlegged ladies with cone hats selling fruit, coconut drinks, *xe oms*, men and boys smoking on their motorcycles parked on the sidewalk. Children coming to our table with stacks of books in their arms; *Lonely Planet* guides to Vietnam, Laos, Cambodia, Graham Greene's *The Quiet American*. They stand silent in front of us until we say no thank you and they move on to the next table.

"I'm okay. Adjusting. It's so hot and noisy. Work is hard." Kelly and I were roommates for seven years in a revolving number of houses in East Vancouver. We have survived friends, lovers, boyfriends, girlfriends, pets and cleaning disputes. One night in Bangkok we shared a room in a hotel. I was living in Japan and had come to travel with him. He cuddled up to me and I froze.

"Kelly! What the hell?"

"I missed you," he said. I removed his hand from my hip and it stayed on the bed the rest of the night.

"The bus to Cui Chi leaves at nine right across the street. You got everything?"

"We don't need much, just some water. I got money changed at the airport."

"What do you think of the city?"

"Cross between Bangkok and India. Except India is worse. Crazy, crazy traffic, people following you around. Traffic here makes Bangkok look slow; it's all the motorcycles. Food's really good. Chicks are pretty cute," he winks at me, crossing his legs, a sandal hanging off his toe.

The bus is already full when we arrive, so the driver pulls out seats that block the narrow aisle and stuffs us all in. Forty of us in a bus that comfortably seats twenty-five. Kelly and I are next to a couple from England, Matt and Lisa.

"What happens if we have to get out? Quickly? We can't *move* in here. And it's so bloody *hot*." Matt complains.

"How do we get out? In an emergency?" Lisa wonders aloud.

"Slowly, I'd say. Slow as hell."

"I hear it's cooler there," Lisa says hopefully, telling

us that they are heading to Hanoi the next day. She is blonde, flushed cheeks, freckled arms. Acid coffee churns in my stomach and the oxygen seems to be all used up. As the bus pulls away from the curb, a group of skinny, beautiful kids kick a deflated soccer ball into traffic, their mothers call out in sharp, staccato voices, call out to passing tourists in loud, listless voices, carry on their chats that sound like arguments, caw of crows. Eyes weary, wary. Pots of soup and noodles at a tiny street café, plastic tables accompanied by tiny plastic stools like furniture from childhood tea parties. Customers slurp, chat, smoke. Wafts of charring meat mixes with exhaust.

The tour guide shuts the flapping doors as we lurch forward into traffic, grabs a crackling microphone as he clears his throat.

"Good…morning. My name is Thanh. It's spelled T- H- A -N -H. It is pronounced 'ton'. Like ton of fun!" He is tall and more solidly built than many other Vietnamese men I have seen, lustrous black hair cut short, slicked back with gel, unlike the usual parted on the side style. His white shirt has a blue and white name tag of the tour company with his name printed in black. T H A N H. *Ton.*

Sweaty heads bob and roll and panic, incited by claustrophobia, tingles up my spine. All I can think about is how do I get off the bus? Even if I could? Where would I go? Wander through the miles of back alleys, be chased by dogs, listen to the screech of karaoke from tiny cement living rooms?

"I spent two years living in America, in California, where I learned English," Thanh continues. His pronunciation is slow but clear, like he is reading a well-practised script, "so I could come back to my country and talk to *you*."

Kelly laughs beside me. "This Thanh guy is pretty funny."

"I was born in Saigon, I am Saigonese. All people from here call Ho Chi Minh City Saigon. We are the workers. Saigon is a lifestyle city. We are going to a residence of war orphans on the way to Cui Chi. These people have lost their family. Or they have lost limbs, or are sick from the war. They are very talented artists."

"How long are we going to be there?" someone asks from the front of the bus. "This stop wasn't mentioned when we bought the tickets."

We start and stop through the centre of the city, streets, sidewalks, alleys are swarming. A few of the sightseers on the bus are munching on sandwiches, the smell of fried eggs in the close heat is overpowering.

Thanh is quick. "Not long at all. They are very talented. We will be there one hour!" And he sits down.

"We will be expected to buy something," Kelly says and Matt nods in agreement. After an hour of slow progress, city thins out, replaced by fields of skinny trees and rice paddies. Oxen pulling ploughs and dots of wide brimmed hats mark farmers, digging, pulling, pushing. When they stand up they still seem bent, like curved wire. Roads turn to gravel and a fine mist of dust floats through the open windows until finally we pull up to a field with a hangar-like building and a few sheds. We file out slow as hell, as Matt predicted, and follow Thanh to the entrance.

"This should be an interesting detour," Kelly laughs. India has taught him to wait, he says. "I have to go every day to the factory or nothing will get done. They're always happy to see me, make tea, chat. I ask how things are going with my clothes, ask to see things and they show me. And I come the next day. Same thing. But if I don't go they will forget about me, not do anything. And I need my shipment by a certain time and they say they will make it for sure. Sometimes they do, sometimes they don't."

"Why do you keep going back?"

"I don't know. It's the way it is."

Hangar is cool, fans swish swish from the ceiling to bring us back to life. The ground and plywood walls are covered with pearl inlaid Vietnamese women, elegant in their *ao dai*, riding bicycles, white fabric flowing, waves of black hair. Young men and women are bent over, sanding wood, painting frames. Some look up and smile at us, hopeful, others completely ignore us. Shelves of black and apple-red lacquered bowls gleam and when I pick them up they seem to float in my hand. Wall hangings dashed with Chinese characters, women crossing a bridge, iconic cone hats.

We file out and Thanh herds us back to the bus. Some of the travellers carry packages wrapped in newspaper.

"Cramming back in our sardine can," Matt says under his breath.

MOSQUITO LAKE

We wake to the sound of rat-a-tat choppers, searchlights beam through sloped tent like some war movie. Nigel thought he was in Vietnam leaving killing fields, wounded hero going home. Clutched guts scrunched fists to his sides, breathed through it. Toby whispers, "Take it easy, Nigel" cold hands on flushed arms. "Choppers will take you to Rupert. Your appendix burst, don't move. You were yelling," Toby says, "you wouldn't stop."

"I saw Lucy drag bodies from the lake," Nigel whispers, "wading through flaming arrows untouched somehow. I called her name from shore but I couldn't move. Marauders threw axes, trees screamed, kept missing her. Canoes capsized, flinging bodies, lake red with blood."

"Don't worry," Toby says. "Lucy saves the lake."

Vietnam

Instead of a movie, Thanh gives a presentation in a square room with scraping wooden chairs that reminds me of Auschwitz, with the exception of whirring fans and the dripping heat. *Swish swish*. Thanh stands beside a diagram of the tunnels, which look like the elaborate paths of ants corkscrewing into the ground. Halls and meeting rooms, kitchens and bedrooms. An entire community subsumed. Through an open door the jungle beckons, thin trees, hillocks, screech of cicadas. Air free of fumes from exhaust, salt and tang of food. Stillness. Thanh uses a pointer that reminds me of my grade two teacher, Mrs. Benner, firm diction, frequent eye contact with the class but with Thanh's distinctive, forceful voice.

"The Viet Cong planned their attacks here." He points to a conference room, square shaped and separate from the other spaces that are round and hovel-like. Expansive heart of the underground village, where all the men met, the soldiers and commanders and generals, drinking, smoking, planning. "People carried on their entire lives underground." *Swish swish*. Part of our group is nodding off to Thanh's tone. Though distinct, it lacks cadence to rouse us from the heat. "They cooked. Raised their children. They even got married. And had a honeymoon. Underground!" He points to a small roundish blob at the far reaches of the community, a private space. "This is where the happy couple spent the first few weeks of their marriage, alone together. They didn't have to work." They were allowed to be happy together before rising to the surface and continuing with life, with the war. But they were fortified, according to Thanh's tone, by love.

He went on some more, said a few things about the Tet Attack, which was planned here as well. But my mind wanders, trying to imagine a life underground. I cannot. But I cannot imagine a war going on above me either. Would I have escaped? Left my home? But to where? War was all around. The Vietnamese dug in, they stood their ground underground, coming up from the depths to maraud in the night like ghosts, like the Terracotta Warriors standing at attention in the ground in China. Except they were alive and fighting, planning, getting married in the dark earth.

DENE

Na'kwoel grew to be so old that his snow-white hair turned yellowish, his knees and elbows were covered with scales that looked like moss. His hearing failed him, and his eyelids drooped until his eyes disappeared. His limbs knotty and swollen, his heart hardening to stone, the earth taking root, claiming him through the soles of his feet. Basking in the sun on a rock or emerging from the shallow water, he would howl in rage at seeing himself ravaged and powerless against time. But he would fight back, exclaiming: Ah, here I am, a young man again!

He was constantly smarting under the pain caused by the untimely death of his eldest son. Though he was now well advanced in years, he used to visit Chichanit's lodge and reproach Chalh'tas with her crime, in which case blows would generally follow words, to all of which she had to submit, though the blows stoked her own rage.

One day, when she was stripping willow bark with a small stone knife, her father-in-law became so violent that, unable to stand his abuse any longer, she grabbed him by the hair, and, throwing him to the ground, stabbed him in the neck. Her knife broke in the old man's collarbone before it could inflict serious injury, and Na'kwoel's screams of pain brought Chichanit running, and he killed Chalh'tas on the spot with his bow point.

Na'kwoel could feel his end coming and he told his people that at the time of his death the mountain Na'kal, which rose on the eastern shore of Stuart Lake, would dance in his honour. It was an agreement he made with the mountain for his long life. A spur of the mountain fell into the water just as he himself fell to the earth.

Vietnam

Finally Thanh leads us to the jungle. There are dark stains under his arms and the line above his lip is beaded. We are guzzling water.

"Do you have more?" Kelly asks.

"Yeah, in my pack." He reaches in and hauls out a warm bottle as we walk. Birds are singing, small black sparrows that hop lightly in front of us. Gunshots ring in the distance. *Rat a tat tat* staccato sounds. We stop at a deep hole in the earth and gather round, looking down at thick pointed bamboo poles waist high, embedded like jaws.

"This is a booby trap!" Thanh proclaims loudly. Air smells like earth, mineral like dried blood. Birds chirp. "This hole would be covered by leaves in the night. And *boom*. An American soldier would fall in. And he would scream in pain. The goal of the Viet Cong was *not* to kill but to maim, to cause pain. Then the other soldiers would hear their friend's cries and come to the rescue and *bam*. The Viet Cong would be waiting in the dark. And they would kill all the soldier's friends that came to help. The plan was to inflict pain, to inflict fear of the night in the American soldiers. They did not know the jungle the way we do." There is pride in Thanh's voice and his eyes flash as he stands there. Gunshots continue, get louder as we follow him.

"What is that?" asks one of the travellers, an edge of nervousness in his voice. He is tall and dark. I hadn't noticed him on the bus. "Oh. There is a shooting range near the canteen. You can shoot machine guns after if you want. AK-47's!"

"Holy shit!" a girl says behind me. Her accent is American, I think. "Guns?"

"Yeah. It's creepy," Kelly replies, turning to check her out. Dirty dog. Stinky smelly Kelly with the jiggly jelly belly.

"God, I need a beer," the tall dark traveller says and the group titters, a little wave of welcome laughter. Unrelenting sun blasting through the thin branches and the meagre dusty leaves. The next booby trap is above ground, a huge net made of fishing line lies dormant on the ground. Once we gather around obediently, Thanh covers the net with leaves, crunchy and dry, mottled green and brown. A few thin vines connect the net to branches overhead, like veins connecting to flesh. From behind a shrub he hauls out a mannequin, a bald plastic sexless body, loose and jangly. He tosses it in a casual heap on the net and WHOOSH the body and net boomerang up to the sky, where it bounces and flails, simulating what would happen to an unsuspecting soldier wandering in the jungle, on the alert for the enemy. Rattle of guns getting closer.

"You see. Another booby trap. American soldier would scream when he got caught and his friends would come. Another ambush. Viet Cong strategy." I am hoping he notices that we are in need of a break, sustenance.

Rat a tat tat. "God it's hot," another girl, English, complains. She is covering her freckled shoulders, which are a raw red, with a scarf.

"Now we will go to the tunnels!" Thanh declares, unflagging in the heat, and we follow him single file through a knot of trees to a clearing with a small hole with a ladder on the edge. Again, we gather around like sheep and it slowly becomes apparent that this tiny aperture is the entrance to the underground world.

"Any volunteers!"

Stunned silence.

"I will." A young man with blond dreads in a blue headband steps forward. I can't place his accent. He's wearing a white t-shirt, long jean shorts and skater shoes.

"Go down and walk through the tunnel to the end," Thanh points to another ladder in the ground, a few hundred feet away. Ground is hard and packed and golden like brown sugar. "What's your name?"

"Chuck!" he calls out, and impossibly disappears down the hole, his hand shoots up as if to surrender.

"The tunnels have been widened for tourists who are taller and bigger than Vietnamese. But you still have to bend over, crouch a little and follow the light to the end."

"There's no way I'm doing this." Panic waves from the soles of my feet, nipping along my thighs, sweat of my spine to the flushed nape of my neck, watching the procession of travellers going down, down into the pit.

"It's what you came for. Come on!" Kelly laughs, giving me a flustered look. "At least try."

I am the last one in line.

Thanh notices my blanched face. "It's okay."

I climb quivering down the stairs and the bird-sounds of the jungle muffle. It's cool. Voices ricochet down the length of the tunnel. Light is immediately eclipsed by the shadow of ground. I make it to the bottom, which is a small enclosure, a mini cloakroom, with four others waiting to enter.

"I don't think I can do this," I say to no one, to all of them.

"Yeah, it's pretty freaky down here," says the comforting voice of a young girl. I can't make out her face, just the outline of her curls. Smells of earth, metallic fear in my mouth. Anxiety claws, ready to tear. At least try. Bodies are clearing out and soon I am the next one to enter the tunnel. I hunch over, make myself into a comma, crunch in and as I move through the walls squeeze. Just keep going. No air, can't breathe. Bodies moving ahead of me, muffled voices make it hard to see the light at the end. What if I can't make it? No one's behind me, I can turn around. Stop for a second. Breathe. Breathe. High-pitched thrum and then nothing. Nothing. Just close your eyes and go. But I don't. I lie down very still and wait for the wave to pass and soon there is no sound at all, just cool air, dirt against my cheek. Heart slows breathing silence. All the people that have passed through here, running, screaming, crying, stealthy, maybe some of them crawled out like I did, hands and knees, hands and knees towards the light.

When I finally haul myself up, Thanh is standing

there. I am the last one, he has been waiting. "You did it. Yay!" he cheers, beaming at me. Everyone else is standing around, drinking water, laughing, lively again. We did what we came for, made it through the tunnel and how awful. In three minutes I combusted to the pressure of fear. Sound floods in and I recover to full, quaking height. Kelly is chatting with Matt and Lisa. I stagger up to them.

"You okay?" Kelly questions, alarmed.

"Yeah."

"Pretty fucking crazy, heh?" Matt explodes. "Can you imagine living down there? *Unbelievable*. Like little bugs scurrying around."

I gather myself together, bit by bit, picking up missing pieces, visible only to me. As we walk towards the canteen, the dummy American GI is lying in the dirt, limbs splayed, its blank face watching our slow procession. I can see the tourists standing in a row, firing at bulls-eye targets through a clearing up ahead. Not so long ago those were soldiers in a jungle with the Vietnamese talking, smoking, planning in the ground, living like rodents. Invisible during the day. At night, cunning marauders.

Japan

After a year in Osaka, I have learned the basics of Japanese from my teacher, Yuki. I started lessons with her when the US invaded Baghdad. I still remember watching the first bombs being dropped, looking up from my notebook, tracing the lines of *hiragana* over and over again, slowly sounding them out. I know how to navigate the myriad train stations by the time I go to Hiroshima. I want to see everything, go everywhere. The exhilaration of learning a new language makes me feel like I am in grade one, shy and insecure, counting numbers with my fingers under the desk. Train travel in Japan is efficient, a smooth ride through the monotonous suburb that is Honshu, bumps of mountains, occasional glimpse of a temple, bright orange gates of a Shinto shrine, cement embanked rivers. Farms, but no animals. I ask my students, "Where are the animals?"

They laugh. "They are inside!"

Shannon and I go with her parents, who are visiting from Canada. They are exhausted from the flight over but want to get to Hiroshima as they are only in Japan for a week, so we take the *shinkansen* the day after they arrive. My students tell me I will love Hiroshima. *It is so beautiful. You must go to Miyajima too, Adrienne san. Floating torii in the sea is very beautiful.* Shannon does not look like her mother. She is small with fine dark curly hair that she has been trying to grow; it swirls in ringlets, popping like corkscrews. Her mother is voluptuous, blonde, worried. *What time are we arriving? Is the hotel near the museum?* Shannon assures, placates. We eat bento boxes we bought at the station, carefully packaged, perfect piles of rice, pickles, thin grilled fish. Salt smell of miso, soya sauce. Train conductor in official blue with white gloves and blue brimmed cap walks calmly through our car, turns around and bows slightly before he moves on to the next car, where he bows again before walking through. Aisles are immaculate, windows shine and we move at the speed of a plane gearing up for takeoff.

We take a taxi from the train station, the driver with immaculate white gloves and blue brimmed cap efficiently packs our luggage in the trunk. I hand him a piece of paper with the address and he nods. Hiroshima is much smaller than Osaka, and greener, my students tell me. The city ranges over craggy hills by the sea, hotels and residential streets fringed with blooming May flowers, the covered shopping streets, *shotengai*, hosting streams of tourists. Cicadas screech in the humidity.

Shannon and I met a few weeks after I arrived in Osaka, became inseparable, sharing a restlessness that brought us here, urging us past the familiar. We had tea every day in the alcove of her long narrow apartment, seated on the floor on silk cushions, leaning out the window to watch women in business suits and high heels ride their bicycles to the train station, talking on their cellphones. *Moshi mosh*? We would complain that there were no men in Japan. Is that why we came? I moved from the suburbs to her apartment building where many teachers lived, which was known as the spaceship, due to its shiny silver exterior. The landlord wore plastic flip-flops and drowned a rat in my bathroom. Occasional giant cockroaches raced down the hallways. We sprayed them with insecticide and took pictures—some had wings and could fly, which was a shock. It was an old building. My next door neighbour was a Buddhist, his chants low and sweet coming through the walls, competing with my electronic music. On my days off I would go to ramen shops, line up with the rest of the customers at the narrow counters, slurp the salty noodles. I would pick a village within an hour's train ride and wander the streets, find a temple I could sit in for awhile and if I was lucky, there would be monks chanting, their wrinkled heads bowed. I learned to kneel in Japan though the bones of my ankles would never quite conform to the hard ground, being reshaped by a new discipline that felt unnatural, exhilarating.

Shannon's stepfather pays the driver. He's tall and lean, friendly, rangy like a corn stalk. Dave and Muriel. They are going to China after this, to see the Terracotta Warriors. Shannon is breezy, bright, summer wildflower. Muriel a potted plant, sturdy, that blooms in the spring.

"The Peace Park is over there." I gesture broadly to the left and no one notices; they're already inside the air-conditioned lobby. A porter dressed in hotel colours, white tailored shirt, blue pants, holds the door for them, his head bowed slightly, hair gleaming blue black.

Our hotel is a few hundred feet from the hypocentre of the atomic bomb. Where it stands was flattened, burned for weeks, bloodthirsty, parched. After dinner Shannon and I walk across a curved stone bridge to the Peace Memorial Park, built on the banks of the Motoyasu River. Dave and Muriel are at the hotel resting. Elegant inscriptions on stone tell us that the park was built on the grounds of Nakajima District, which contained seven towns and 6,500 people, most of whom perished in the bombing. The district is about the size of the village I grew up in. A round mound rises up on our right, a grey concrete pagoda resting at the crest, holding the ashes of 70,000 unclaimed or unknown bodies. Elegant hotels with balconies, streetside cafés and shops, puffs of shrubs and trees watch over the park. A-bomb Dome is a shambling dinosaur, the only wreck left standing after the incineration. Majestic and eerie, a sign says it was built by a Czech designer and is a World Heritage site. Blasted window frames like eye sockets, dark, immobile. A river eases past.

Blue green white yellow red delicate cranes folded in sharp pointed angles and tied together in long strings drape over natural stone monuments, dedicated to villages, schools and workers wiped out at the hypocentre. A three-pronged sculpture in the shape of a bomb with a young girl standing atop, arms stretched wide to hold the shape of a bronze crane. Imposing arc-shaped cenotaph at the heart of the park keeps the names of 221,893 souls safe in a chest and fountains spray tonnes of water a minute to quench thirsty souls. Behind the A-bomb

Dome there are hundreds of cranes hanging in bushes, made by school children from all over Japan, a sign says, in the hopes that a disaster of this magnitude will never happen again

How many bodies are buried here? Bones, ashes beneath pavement, deep in the ground. All the signs say the souls are resting and they may be. The park is peaceful. Families, knots of friends seem to float by as if on some invisible, calm breeze. Teenagers sit on the edge of the river where the grass is soft and nubby, chatting and smoking. Some girls wear the classic school uniform: boxy blue blazers, short blue pleated skirts and white leggings past their knees. Jagged, straight glossy hair. A boy with dark blocky glasses and rolled-up grey jeans sits alone, listening to music through headphones. Air smells like green buds, fresh and lemony.

Walking the circumference of the park, monuments pop out pale like ghosts from the trees and shrubs. Severe grey concrete monoliths ribboned with strips of *kanji*, natural stone standing bold, unmovable. Sculpted willowy woman with a delicate deer by her side. Lion's head fountain spouts continuous streams. Coins glint through the clear water. We find a bench, share a smoke. As the sun goes down, the shadows from the A-bomb Dome steal across the grass, part of the river, the holes of windows blacken so no light gets out at all.

Glow of cigarettes spark the night. We don't leave right away. It's cool, the flutter of voices and bark of laughter punctuates the black. Birds flit, sing to each other. Stillness sets my legs straight out, toes hanging out of my sandals, even they feel relaxed, weary after cramped crunching on trains and taxis. Puff of pot floats by, aromatic.

"Smells good. Should we crash that party, track down the smoke?"

"Nah. They don't want to hang out with *gaijin*."

"I could get some for your mom. I think Muriel needs a puff."

"My mom is driving me crazy. I wish she would relax."

"She's worried about you. God knows why."

We don't move for awhile, pass cigarettes back and forth. Breeze picks up, flips my hair around, and we curve to the hard slats of the bench beneath us. It is inscribed with the name of Naoto Yamamoto, a respected teacher and former resident of Nakajima. She was forty-three when she died.

DENE

Allied to Na'kwoel's family was brooding Tsalekulhye, the first of a line of hereditary chiefs, whose family came from Pinche, a village on Stuart Lake. Born about 1735, he was younger than A'ke'toes, whose sister or cousin he must have married, since his eldest son ultimately succeeded to A'ke'toes rank.

Some members of the northern Sekanais tribe made a friendly visit to the Stuart Lake band. One evening there was a scream in the camp, and one of the Sekanais saw his own sister bleeding to death from an arrow wielded by Tsalekulhye. Narrow eyes, keen rage, Sekanais shot Tsalekulhye as he crept to the woods. Angry arrow gouged his thigh. He recovered his strength but the wound sunk deeper, malicious. Notorious story passed like poison at fires, tribe to tribe and his fear and pride grew—no one would cross him or his family.

About the year 1780, a beloved member of the Naskhu'tin tribe died near the confluence of the Blackwater and Fraser. Grief flooded the ears of a shaman who said that Tsalekulhye killed him. Twisted bitter Tsalekulhye, he said, and the Naskhu'tins despair sickened to wrath, and they gathered their rage in arms to Stuart River, in search of Tsalekulhye.

Japan

Next morning Jack Johnson's mellifluous voice breezes in the background of the café. *On and on, on and on, on and on ...* Dave and Muriel seem to have recovered, clear eyed, buttering their toast. Muriel looks at Shannon intently, as if trying to glean some secret she knows the answer to. Best to be quiet, her firm even mouth seems to say. When Shannon told Muriel she was going to Japan, her mother slapped her, marked her cheek like claws.

"Coffee's good! So girls, what's the plan?" Dave is handsome when he smiles.

An efficient waitress dressed in a faux Dutch uniform with an elaborate hat that looks like a folded diaper clears our table. She smiles, "Good morning!"

"Museum and then Miyajima in the afternoon," I answer. Shannon is texting on her phone.

"Will we have time?" Muriel is hunched in her seat. The room is yellow, bright, stuffy, smells like sweet bread.

I am not rested. Even with the air-conditioning I woke in a sweat and stared at the blank grey ceiling which was screening an internal war movie, wooden forts being defended, gunshots and whizzing axes. I watched daylight seep in white ghost fingers. Shannon didn't move in the next bed.

"Yeah, we should," Shannon answers curtly, flips her phone. "Let's get going."

Our café is in a *shotengai*, a covered shopping street. In Osaka, the *shotengai* at Namba feels like a surging carnival, a colourful roving shopping breathing being. Hiroshima crowds don't run in the same numbers and it feels like being in an atrium, rounded opaque awnings giving off refracted greenish light.

Irashaimase! Irashaimase! Beautiful young girls in shops call out to us.

"It means *welcome*," I say to Dave, who is walking beside me. Muriel and Shannon are in heated debate behind us. I can hear Shannon hiss, then yell "*No!*"

"Mothers and daughters," Dave says lightly and laughs.

We are nearing the end of the tunnel where the park opens up, a Saturday morning moving, milling landscape, groups of families festive with portable karaoke machines. Bash of drums and slash of guitar—two or three impromptu jam sessions crank the air. One singer is swivelling his hips like Elvis, his hair in a slick pompadour, bright red lipstick.

Dave is delighted. Muriel takes pictures of the A-bomb Dome, asks us to stand in front of it. Cacophony seems to have erased the mood of last night. Earthy aroma of roasted nuts, moss-coloured *matcha* ice cream. We follow the crowds to the museum.

"What were you guys talking about?" I ask Shannon, as I dodge a huge pink Hello Kitty balloon.

"She wants me to come back home, get a job teaching in Toronto."

"Why? You're teaching now."

"That's what I told her. She's never happy. Wants what she wants, you know? She was like that with my dad too." Shannon's father is remarried and lives in China with his second wife.

The museum is grey, sprawling blocks, flat-roofed, like a spread-out accordion, slatted sections with brief black windows. At the entrance a picture of licking flames takes up the entire wall. Orange red yellow daubs and gashes. Spattered spilled and splayed like flesh.

"That was painted by a survivor," says the cashier brightly and hands me my ticket.

Inside there's a slab of stone emblazoned with the shadow of an incinerated body. Those closest to the hypocentre combusted instantly, leaving black imprints and ash. Behind glass, torn and burned school uniforms, books, crushed eyeglasses. Framed letters from the Japanese government pleading for an end to the war. Pictures painted by survivors of naked bodies, tongues bursting. There was no water. Thirst was so intense that people threw themselves in wells, off bridges into the river circling the park. Skin peeling off in whole sheets like puff pastry. Accounts from the survivors, translated, etched in vellum, accompanied by broad charcoal strokes of leaning naked bodies.

As we near the end, Shannon realizes that we've lost Muriel and we backtrack to find her sitting on a bench, weeping. We circle her, shielding her from stares. Dave is as shocked as we are.

"I don't know," she cries in a high voice that croaks in a sob. "I can't imagine how horrible it would be to lose…" People pass by, too polite to stop but I can tell they're listening. "To lose a child. How horrible." We are near the exhibit with the children's clothes, blasted book covers.

"Muriel, you're exhausted. Let's go back to the hotel," says Dave. She doesn't look at any of us, pulling her face together after its collapse, determined, smoothing out wrinkled thoughts.

"No. Let's go to the island. I need to get out of here." Grown-up voice again with forced cheer, which does not inform her weary walking. Shannon hands her a napkin to dry her eyes.

"What a place," Dave says as we walk toward the bridge to our hotel, hoping to open up the conversation, deflect from the outburst. He may have a knack for making light of things. Path is less crowded than when we came, the bands have packed up.

"It was grim," I say, thinking of all the survivors, talking to translators, the wrenching of words, images seared to their insides. Primal, unbearable heat. "How can you not remember it and carry on?"

"I guess you cannot not remember," Shannon adds. We stop for *matcha* ice cream. "Does that make any sense?" We laugh but it takes awhile to shake it off, like the morning after a bad dream, wanting the familiarity of your room to crowd out the unrest that came from somewhere. A little boy's jacket, a little girl's skirt.

DENE

The Carriers were camped in three large detachments on the upper course of the Stuart River. The southern-most tribe was the first to hear the swarming news—a large force of Naskhu'tins was on its way up to avenge its dead. Tsalekulhye knew that his name was on their blackened lips, painted on their war faces. Fear forced him to the lower encampment.

Frightened and doubtful that they could fight off the warriors, the southern tribe decided to move up and join the other two allied bands. But a heavy snowstorm came on, delayed their departure and a great cry was raised on the top of the bank. The Stuart Lake people were hunted with whizzing arrows, spears flying, war-clubs stunning right and left. Such hideous yells of attack. Two headmen were slain and mutilated, the marauders kept coming. Most of the women were taken as prisoners, enslaved. Tsalekulhye, the cause of the disaster, took to the water, and was on the point of escaping when he was recognized, killed and pulled apart.

JAPAN

We get directions to Miyajima from Kimi, a clerk at our hotel. She has very thin, fine hair that frames her narrow face, tiny curved shoulders huddled in a cardigan, her narrow fingers point at the red *torii* on the map and trace backwards to our hotel. A streetcar will take us there. We catch it here, and she points to a tiny spot in a myriad of lines, marks it with her pink pen.

"You will find it, no problem," she smiles.

"Can we take the map?"

"Of course," and she hands it to me, bows slightly.

Although Shannon and I are famous for getting on the wrong trains and not noticing for several stops—stories which we regaled her mother with—we are allowed to do the navigating. Probably because Dave and Muriel don't want to think.

"Things all cleared up now?" I ask.

"Who knows? What's with the public meltdown? Is she trying to guilt me?"

From the immaculate streetcar windows Hiroshima peeps out in carefully cultivated beauty, flashes of tankers on a choppy sea. New housing areas open up outside the downtown core, chunks of ripped-up earth covered over quickly in concrete, paved roads. Tiny perfect cars in the driveways. We pass a school that is playing children's songs on the outdoor PA system, high-pitched clear voices float through some open windows. In my guide book the Shinto temple on Miyajima is built on wooden pillars, resting on the lap of the sea.

"We should go for a swim," I suggest to Shannon. I want to get away from Dave and Muriel. It has been uncomfortable being in a family dynamic that is not my own.

Streetcar weaves and climbs stubbled green hills. Industrious caterpillar about to shed its passengers at the ferry dock. Gaggle of girls giggle at the back, light tittering laughter. Afternoon heat dumbs us down. Muriel is sleeping in her seat.

"Great idea. They can shop for awhile."

My legs are sticking to my seat and I have to slowly unglue them. The ferry is a welcome, breezy boat and I lean over the metal railing, trying to catch a glimpse of the *torii* like some beacon. My guidebook says the *torii* is a traditional Japanese gate most commonly found at the entrance of a Shinto shrine. It symbolizes the transition from the profane to sacred.

Salt air reminds me of home and for a moment sadness mars the moment; I want the familiar, to feel snug instead of wide open.

Ferry grunts and puffs and sways off to the island and when we arrive the *torii* is as magical as the book says, floating on the sea though its foundations go deep. Shinto shrine has light tatami rooms that smell like wheat, lined up against each other like secret compartments. Incense circles in the corners. We walk on the wooden slats, bright orange beams reflect off Shannon's sunglasses in blobs.

"Think about walking out here every morning with your java!" I say, enchanted.

We find some concrete steps that we can jump off of near a little beach at the end of the shopping street. A well-dressed little boy is picking up pebbles, dropping them in his mother's lap, one by one.

"We can change into our suits at a restaurant bathroom when we have lunch."

"Does anyone swim here? I don't see anyone swimming? What if we're not allowed to?" Suddenly Shannon is apprehensive.

We have to go swimming, I've decided that it is necessary at this time to feel clean. The shopping street on the island is an elegant shanty town selling rice cakes, ice cream, paper fans painted blue green outlining thin white cranes. Smell of roasted sesame seed, a dry green mixed with salt.

"Come on. No one will stop us. What will they do?"

Water laps past my knees and the roundish stones rub my feet. The *torii* looms in front of me and I think briefly of swimming to it. Shannon is splashing beside me, "Water, water everywhere and not a drop to drink," she calls out to me. Sounds recede and I think of the Shinto priests listening to the rush and suck of water as they go to sleep, when they wake up. From here, there is no Hiroshima, just the mountainous island behind us, the jagged Japanese coast where a warlord decided to build a city. When the water reaches the bottom of my chin, I submerge myself and then let the salty sea lift me back up, resting my feet above water. Blue sky opens up, unbounded, swirls of greyish cloud like smoke drift past the horizon and show up, I am sure, on the other side of the world, which would be home.

In Search of Mosquito Lake

We are late starting, morning spent with items crossed off lists, chocolate smeared from breakfast muffins. At the hardware store we buy a lantern when we really need a camp stove. Sarah says we can cook over a fire, she has a special recipe that requires a can opener, tins of tomatoes, wieners in thin plastic wraps.

"People really do eat anything when they are hungry," I say. I am always hungry. Intense impatience accelerates metabolism to the speed of sound.

Owner of the store smiles as he lights the wick, immediate light and hiss draws the attention of a Mennonite boy at the till. Stands by his father, both with hands deep in their pockets, handmade pants, black strap suspenders. From another era, the silent screen. Round black hats on smoothed hair, father has a chaotic beard, horn-rimmed glasses, watches rapt as his son. Owner smiles, beatific—we are his lost flock, he has found us in the corner, hiding from the light. I give Sarah a nudge. We need to catch the three o'clock ferry or there is no use going at all.

"Let's roll!" I hiss. Enthralled with her new lantern, she asks the owner if it gives off a lot of heat. Can I burn it inside my cabin? Does it give off toxic fumes? He is a fisherman, classic in Shetland sweater, Irish flat cap nesting on his grey curls. Lined, kind face. He hasn't answered yet, one of his employees has elbowed in. Mennonite father and son are still staring, motionless. They live halfway between Masset and Port Clements. I've seen their homestead, unlovely clearing, sheared sheep wandering across the road. Solid house shuddering in all that space.

We leave finally, questions unanswered, lantern stuffed in the box, jammed in the back with the gear, surrounded by pillows. It can't break, Sarah says. It cost fifty bucks and I don't want to buy another one. Finally at the ferry terminal, morning mash of harried shopping and I wanted to get here much sooner. Fifteen years ago I lived in the bush, picked mushrooms, bathed once a week, smelled like dirt and ferns. Every day hauling buckets up and over the waves of hills. Skinny and tough, I lit these lanterns every night, frozen calloused fingers flicking one mouldy Bic after another. Often the sound startled me as I turned the wick down.

Moresby is mounds of grey light, lumps of deep green. Impenetrable. Sleeping in the van I would open my eyes to black night. Frost slowly dancing on the window. Ferry docks and unloads, sloshing in the bay, open deck cleared in minutes. Deckhands head to smoking spots, slouched, one hand in their pockets to keep warm. Wall of cold wind cushions them, they lean into it. They could be the same guys from last time, grown up, with homes and families on one side or the other.

Yellow mesh fence is removed and cars, trucks hunch in, slick-backed like beetles. Rock a bit, water-sloshed moors. Salt driven slap blasts as we get out, wander to the edge. Seagulls gasp, belligerent. Other motorists are reading newspapers, drinking coffee in white cups, oblivious, heads bowed over their steering wheels.

Tall ferryman with walrus moustache joins us, cigarette smoke streaming through dragon nostrils.

"You girls camping?" Appraising eyes, slow amused voice.

Sarah says yeah, we're going to Mosquito Lake. Ferryman raises quizzical eyebrows, exhales. Could be cold. You got rain gear?

Deep-throated engine chugs out the periphery of voices. I lean over the edge, try to glean the swim of seals, their curious eyes. Sarah takes pictures of everything, focused, refocused, refracted light-framed beauty. Such beauty, she says, needs more light. I wait for something to surface, for the sea to offer up a gift.

I can't remember how to get there, I yell to her in the wind. She can't hear, is open to the picture world but I need to fling it out there. Less fear then. Ferryman sidles up, he's heard me. Blue-eyed and smiling, he speaks in snippets that the wind can't snatch. There's only one road. Follow it. Sign to Mosquito Lake says go left past Skidegate Lake. Drive careful, potholes are deep, will blow out your tires. Logging's done so there's not a lot of traffic, could be walking a bit if you do. So stock up on water, fuel for fire. SuperValu in Sandspit is open till eight. I thank him, hands clutching the railing to steady the roll.

Shore comes up and we huddle back, pilgrims on to the next vista. Up the steep ramp and rounded curves and there is Sandspit, flung out, grey, hinging on at the edge of the world, boarded windows, for sale signs with black marker numbers to call, please call. Looks like logging took the money out. Waves polish stones like candy on the shore. People move in the mould and green wet, steady, hunch over their gardens, prune their trees. Held by the constant line of the horizon.

There's the trailer park where I had my weekly shower, I show Sarah. It looks the same. Red Roof restaurant with the excellent pizza. I drive past SuperValu to the airport so Sarah can see the whole place, the cedar hotel with the Haida gift shop. Engine that keeps the town going, fitful heartbeat.

Pulling in to the mini-mall with the grocery store, men in work boots are chatting at open windows, diesel idling revs through me. Second-hand store is open, Sarah squeals, she loves second-hand shops, flies out the door, dashes across the gravel. SuperValu is the hub of Moresby—post office, liquor store, car parts. In a small aisle by the spirits, there's beer, rows of wine. I grab a six-pack for the road.

How do I get to Mosquito Lake, I ask, squinting at a map behind the cashier. Measured look through glare of glasses, long dyed brown hair, no shine, frizzy bangs. Here's where you are now, she says. Sparkles on her index finger, long nail arched. Turn left at the school, road runs to gravel at the edge of town. You'll pass the old fishing camp, cross a few bridges. When you get to Skidegate Lake, keep going, turnoff's on your left. Rapid fire, direct, she knows everything. What people drink, what they eat, sharp eyes see the insides. There is only one road, she repeats the ferryman. Drive slow.

One dollar shades! Sarah slips in beside me, beaming about her deal. Catches the last part of the conversation—one road, drive slow—and I walk to the car, buckled knees from some deep driving current, cold, cold feet. Maybe a beer will help. Sarah rides shotgun and we turn at the school, camera attached, extended eye.

Pavement eases to gravel and we are bouncing along, just like we did in the van, dust fuming through the vents. It was always sunny and I was always happy in the memory. Food and wine in boxes, my hair untangled and benign down my back. At a turn off we keep going, trees bending branches into open windows and I panic again. Do I remember? Try to discern the pull.

Crack a can of beer, pass one to Sarah. Late afternoon sun casts its mellow light on her cat's eye frames. Road is empty and we start counting off the miles. 1 ... 2 ... 3. Without logging, so quiet, no blasting trucks to watch out for. We could be the only ones here for miles. Fishing camp pops up, cottages crowded by the rocky shore.

Let's get out, take a look around, Sarah says, laughing, her long hair octopus twirling. Sometimes she wears it in a wreath. Almond eyes, broad round cheeks. She just finished a year of law school in Toronto. Not sure she wants to be a lawyer, or how she will be when she comes out. Snarled and tense or unravelled. We met at a guest house her first day in Masset and she already knew the way to the beach. We walked past a moss-shrouded graveyard. One grave was entirely covered in gleaming pink alabaster, fragile sea skins.

On a white board on the side of a decaying cabin are drawn lines of a round-robin tournament with names carefully printed in black. Moresby Coho Salmon Derby, 2007.

That was four years ago, she says and takes a picture like it will change. Some of the cabins are listing, others have been lifted up on new beams, smell of fresh wood. Clean windows, drawn curtains. Does anyone live here? I look again at the neat rows of names that have survived pelting rainstorms. Sarah goes to the beach for another view, leaving me in the stillness. Watch the windows, she says, look for a flutter. I wait and there is nothing. Maybe they are in town, buying beer, I call out to Sarah. I walk to the beach. She is hunched over pools of anemones, snapping them as they close their tentacles around slippery seashells, alive and hungry.

I don't really know where I'm going, so I'm hoping I'll remember, I tell her, calmed this time by a few beers. Sun is out, dappling the pocked road. That's part of the adventure, Sarah says as we ease through the deepest holes. When we reach Mile 13 we stop again. Road is decaying but signs are fresh, black lettering, yellow squares pop out at each bend. This is where the ghost chased us out, I say. She already knows my stories. In Masset, we talk late to candlelight, green tea, coffee at the tiny warm cinnamon shack when it's open. Sip from thick potted mugs. Peering through the brush at the side of the road, thin trees drink deep, light gets darker. Can't see the ridge from here, seems flatter. No trails in that I can see. But they're there, they always are, paths remembered by the worn earth.

So, is it speaking to you? She asks when I get back in. Mosquitoes pounce dumbly on the windows. No. I could hang out a bit but it's getting dark, I say. She takes pictures of me posing, silly, fake serious. Interesting part is the light, I say, how green it is.

Fifty thousand shades of green! Sarah exclaims.

At least! I slurp on another beer.

Car develops a cough and rattle, like it is old and choking on the past. It wheezes but when I mention it, Sarah says she can't hear anything. Giant white head, proud eagle gleams through branches and Sarah says *stop*. Urgency leaves her when she gets out, quietly inching on the road. Eagle is by a fierce clear creek. At the bridge she catches it before it sweeps away on dinosaur wings.

Mile 25... 26... 27. Lake looms at the edge, left-hand side of the road. That must be it I say to Sarah. Feist is playing on the blown-out stereo. ... *February, April says*... There's a pull-in by the lake where people camp, a launch for boats. Clear-cuts shear the mountains rolling on the other side. We get out, lake is calm, loons in the middle bow gracious heads, concealing their sorrow.

Is this Mosquito Lake? I say to Sarah. She is framing me, careful to catch the clouds trailing the trees reflecting on the water. Bulrushes push up their thick brown heads. I remember going across this lake in a blow-up boat, I say. We got it at the hardware store, same place you got your lamp. Same guy sold it to us. We thought we would go pick on the other side, see what was there. Everything around here had been over-picked or claimed. There were fights about territory over camp-fires, so we thought: go further, cross the lake. Paddles were blue plastic, wind carried us over and it's smaller than it looks, this lake. Other side is steep, mushrooms were rotted mostly. We were too late. Got soaked in a storm on the way back.

What happened to the boat, Sarah says. We are walking to the other side of the road. There is a post and beam structure for a lean-to left by some campers. Bits of plastic cling to pounded-in nails. Charred bits of wood surrounded by scorched stones. Been awhile since anyone's stayed here, I say. It is so quiet, except for buzzing bugs. Breeze flurries the leaves, they shine luster and silver. Don't remember about the boat, it was cheap, maybe we sold it before we left.

Should we keep going? I say. Lady in the store says the turn-off for Mosquito Lake is left. Although this could be Mosquito Lake. I can't remember but I know I've been here before.

She said the turn-off is on the left-hand side, Sarah repeats. I can't read her eyes through the sunglasses, but she is fine to keep going.

So we crest a hill that snakes around the lake. Weeds crowd out the shallow end, swallow up the water to make more land, change the landscape. Hill turns to mountain, keeps going. I really don't know where I am now, I tell Sarah. Crack another beer, which has turned warm in the sun. Feist is singing *secret heart, what are you afraid of* and Sarah has found a bag of chips to tide us over. We crunch them back and forth.

On a straight stretch, bob of a tiny tail, a baby deer wobbling down the road. Delicate legs, awkward gait that speeds up in terror at the sound of us, our presence and no mother around. Panicked, it doesn't know where to go, even as it picks up speed. Sarah is enthralled and we stop for a picture although I want to leave. We should pass it by, I say. Side of the bank is too steep to climb so it sinks into some brush by the road. So small that it will be invisible, letting the earth shield it so we walk by. Sarah gets in close, deer shivers, is shaking, white spots like dips of paintbrush grazing brown skin, nose wet, eyes closed tightly, thick fringe lashes. Bones so small, like bent grass.

Hurry up, I say. I can't watch this. It's going to explode from fear right by the side of the road. Mile 47 pops out when I look ahead. What mile was it that our camp was at? Must have passed it, land didn't look like this. Memory scoured, comes up empty.

We settle in and go for the hundredth time. This reminds me of Sisyphus, stone rolling up, stone rolling down, I say as I start the ignition. Tires are holding out so far, I checked them, gave them a little kick. I watch the baby deer in the rear-view mirror while Sarah checks her pictures. It is still in the bushes, waiting. It doesn't flinch.

Dene

Tsalekulhye had four brothers, the youngest, fifteen, named Nathadilhthouelh, found his sister and brother hiding by the river and he loaded them on his back. Hot tears shedding on his shoulders, he started to cross the river. One foot at a time, steady through pummelling current. Need to be strong, he begged them, we all need to be strong, no screaming. Sister is eight, brother is three and they lock onto him. Transformed, all their skin clutching, he thought they could make it. Then the current loosened their grip. The cold, the fear was too much. But he didn't let them go. They were taken. Body wracked in sobs, he reached the shore naked. Another sister ran along the border of ice clinging to the shore. He screamed keep going, keep going. Out of reach of hostile eyes and arrows, he stood on the shore of the doomed camp waiting for the end of the massacre.

In Search of Mosquito Lake

Road rounding, swerving around potholes, all the beer is gone and we are facing the sea. Last few miles I took every left turn, searching for a sign that said Mosquito Lake. Losing light, hunger edges in and we are dragging rotting branches and tinder twigs to start a fire, haul out the boxes, tins, spread out the tent. Beat the bugs back with slapping hands.

"Is this a good spot to spend the night?" Sarah pounds pegs into pliant earth.

"Campsite has been used before, you can tell by the clearing," I zip up the flap, snug against cool evening.

"Where the hell are we?" I plop down on the rocks. Sarah stirs dinner, a bubbling pan of goo, pail of water rolls and steams for tea. Tide comes up and we rush to save our things but it only grazes the beached tree that shields us, becomes our table and couch. Rocky islet hovers at the edge of the bay, water rushing over its edges, trying to smooth past the opening, held by silver horizon.

"Some kind of inlet," Sarah keeps stirring. "We can check on the map tomorrow."

"How did we miss it?" Only one road and we fucking missed it.

Plan was to spend the night at Mosquito Lake, test

the story, see if spirits still rise up from the land, bent on revenge. I take pictures of her hunched over, feeding the fire. On a wander down the beach, I find a newspaper open, travel section of wide beach in crystalline Asia. I may have even been there once but it's too dark to read the print. I pick it up, bring it back to burn. Trucks hauling boats and families roll by to camp on another shore. Dim glow of lighthouse starts like a firefly, grows sharp in the darkness, reaching out to ships we will never see.

There's a wire frame person perched on a deck, I tell Sarah. Some yellow house by the sea in Queen Charlotte. You can see through it. It's cut in half by grass and stones but the outline is a person. Someone must have made it, like they wanted a watcher, a companion or something. It's strange. I look at it every time I walk by.

Sarah looks at me, smiles. There is a boy she is talking about, two boys; one here, one in Toronto. One here is dreadlocked, dreamy. She is trying to figure them out, reading between the lines of texts. They don't compare to the boy that caught her heart when she was young, though, she tells me. He swims in her still. Water is heating for dishes, which is my job. Branches snap in the woods by us, tripped over by deer.

There's also this young woman who plays loud heavy metal every morning on my way to work, I continue. She wanders in and out of her cabin, a flaming sun tattoo on her arm, surrounded by all that disruptive quiet.

"God, her neighbours must hate her," Sarah laughs. All the other homes are quaint, seaside village out of a picture. I love the walk, mountains of Moresby filling in the edges, adding heft. Always something that sticks out, she says. Things that don't seem to fit.

Hard to see the stars by the fire and smoke so I walk down the road a bit before it gets too dark. Blooming June trees climb the rocks to rest in an odd quiet. Sea lisps in the background. I only go so far, some part of me stops in the road, says this is it. Invisible line, internal horizon makes its claim. Back at the fire Sarah is reading Haida myths.

"An elder in Masset said she hears the voices of her ancestors all the time, hears their canoes crunch up on the shore," she says as she closes the book. Sarah works in Old Masset, rides her bike from the new village to the old every day, wind trying to blow her off the road, or at least it feels like it. Until her legs got stronger, she tells me. Weathered totem poles stand in front of houses, tell their stories. I wonder what the houses of our ancestors looked like, I say. Where were the stories carved? Who knows, she says. Maybe they were made with strings and wire to carry things instead. Fire transforms the wood, night huddles in close.

Dawn and I wake, all my clothes on, sleeping bag zipped but I'm compelled to get up. Make sure the tide isn't threatening our camp, leave us safe for a calm breakfast. Freezing, I dig in the car for my phone. It is too early to be up. There is no service out here, passed over by careening satellites. Standing still on the road, lighthouse has become firefly again.

After breakfast we pack up and head back to Skidegate. Can't remember when the ferry leaves. Road looks different on the way back, shock of memory pulls me over to a waterlogged lane. Ahead is a bridge cobbled of decaying logs, crossing to the other side of lake we passed yesterday. Be careful when you cross, I call to Sarah. There are spots where you can drop through if you aren't looking. She traipses ahead, triumphant, she has spotted deep brown deer eyes nestled in the swamp grass. My feet follow the greened-over logging road that trails the lake. Peach heads of mushrooms clump by the road.

I remember walking down this road, I call over my shoulder to her, but she has disappeared. Bulrushes stalk the shore. Logging has shorn this side of the lake of understorey, easier to see the paths we followed, back-tracking with full pails. Corey leading the way, eager to find money mushrooms, rounded rare pines pickers shot each other over in Terrace camps. Stories of these skirmishes spread at campfires—they're worth a thousand bucks in Japan, an aphrodisiac. Disbelieving, shocked voices.

Branches frame the road, scenic painting, sun warms the gaps in trees. No breeze ruffling the corners that could lift to some other lurking time, its breath coming in waves, beating the earth. Sarah shows up, says there's an old mill I need to see, shambling into the lake. Some pickers came here on bikes, I tell her. Pails strapped on the front and back, looked apocalyptic, like the end of the world: we'll all be on bikes with pails, foraging for food. She frames me in front of the mill, which doesn't look like anything now, a pile of logs fading from its function. We wander back, share a bag of trail mix, squirrels' hard acorns thunk beside us. *Tchock tchock* of watching raven.

Other end of Skidegate Lake, miles start counting down—44, 43, 42. Way back seems shorter. Day of watching the green unfold, eyes following old logging roads, defunct trails has rattled the part that remembers. I swerve sharply again, this time to the right, just past mile 16. Get out and scramble under blowdown blocking the road and I know it. This is the road we lived on, the one that started off bold and then couldn't make up its mind at a crossroads past a rotting bridge. One road climbed a steep cliff and the other down a ravine. Neither one went very far.

I walked down this road every morning to wake up, breaking the icy puddles with my boots, I call to Sarah as I pick up speed. We dodge more blowdown. It hasn't been used in awhile. She has caught up with me, flushed, and I reach the small bereft clearing. It used to feel cozy, I tell her. Log bridge that led to other roads has washed out. I used to cross it and sit in the sun where the roads parted ways, felt like I was held by the blowing grass.

I check in the woods for logs and timber that campers may have stowed. When we left, we dragged everything we used to make camp and covered the pile with a few tarps for the next year. Thought we would be back. There is nothing stored that I can see. Maybe the last campers burned everything. Sarah has climbed down to the twisting cold, cold stream. Deep brown from the moss and leaves, it stained dishcloths, tea towels but it washed the sweat off. Hopping from roots to stones, crossing the stream, I find the small clearing where I bathed. It looks just as I left it, I say to Sarah. Surge of joy, I want to mark it. *This is the spot where I stood.* But I don't. It is enough to be here again, to have found my way to a place I wasn't looking for.

It is 2:00 p.m. by the time we get back to Sandspit and we rush to the hotel to check the ferry schedule. There is a three o'clock that we must catch, so Sarah can find a ride on the ferry back to Masset. Probably lots of people heading that way, says the young man at the gift shop. He shakes our hands, says he is Gabriel. Shows us argylite carvings of whales curved on pins, glistening shells for fins. Rows of silver, thunderbirds, frogs with long tongues lick the rims of rings. He has worked here every summer for the last four years and is from Skidegate. Gentle voice, he doodles on paper while he waits for customers.

He gets out a map, the same one that was at Super-Valu, but it looks different. We trace our journey with dirty fingers. Gabriel returns with hot coffee from the hotel café.

"This is it, the place where we stayed last night, I think," Sarah says.

"Where is Mosquito Lake?" I ask, and Gabriel shows us the road we missed.

The lake you passed is Skidegate Lake, he said. That is where the mushroom pickers gather every year, not as many as there used to be. The clearing by the lake is where the buyers' tents are set up.

"So that was Skidegate. I knew I had been there, but I thought it was Mosquito," I say, coffee warmth flooding me and some deep release. I could lean on the counter and sleep.

Sarah and Gabriel try to figure out the exact spot we stayed, they have it narrowed down. The lighthouse places us at the northern tip, Gabriel says, close to the open ocean. I don't know it very well but I've been by there.

"You've been so helpful," we say, and thank him before heading back to the car. Sun comes out to bask in for a few minutes before we have to go.

DENE

Chinlac chief Khadintel was a respected man who had two wives and told stories of his ancestors to his many children. Strong warrior, brave, a graceful dancer. He had killed an equally respected warrior from the Chilcotin clan some time back. Chinlac villagers heard rumours of revenge, of marauders who would come to the village. They talked about it with fear, like a coming storm. What would they do when the avengers arrived? They prepared, made bows and arrows and armour, waves of the choppy lake slapped the bottoms of their repaired canoes. They prayed and waited, hoping that the reprisal would not come. And then one day the marauders came, a large group of Chilcotin warriors paddling in from the south, armed and ready in sturdy canoes.

Return to Mosquito Lake

Years later I am in muggy Toronto, drinking wine in Sarah's kitchen on a street of red brick houses. Dragging my rolling suitcase from the subway in the dark, every house looks the same, I tell her. I had to stop to peer at the numbers to make out the right place. Spring is so early I can wear light dresses, sit on patios before I head home—not like the north where buds are still hard knots in branches. When she opens the door there are fitted dresses on hangers she can slip into for work. One more year and she needs to article but she may do her master's, teach instead. I can hear in her voice that she does not want to change, to go out into the world firm, pressed and suited.

When you left Queen Charlotte after our trip, it was just me and my beach house, she said. Such a cold summer, I had to build a fire every night but I got good at it. Figured out the stove, kept the smoke out. Went deep-sea fishing, just me in the waves and the old men were so kind, let me keep a fish. It kept me full for a week. Mom was supposed to visit before I left in August, but it didn't happen, so I went to Gwaii Hanaas. She brings out chocolate, bars of it and I choose the dark one. Kitchen is small, glow of Tiffany-style lamp on the round table. Deck in the back is ready for plants to grow.

The bus to Moresby was full of tourists from Germany,

Holland, thick accents and smiles, she tells me. I didn't see the turn-off or the sign but the tour guide announced Mosquito Lake. I jumped out of my seat, ran up to him and said stop the bus. I need to take a picture of Mosquito Lake. He looked at me and the tourists laughed and I gave him my charming smile. He said okay, be quick, so I ran out and took pictures and it looked just like you said. It was stormy that day, couldn't see the tip of the mountain by the lake, too much fog but I felt something there. I didn't want to stay.

I learned how to be alone that summer, she tells me. My relationship with the earth kept away gloomy thoughts, sharp eyes pointed at me. It was a hard place to be, there were people around but I didn't always connect with them. I was trying to keep warm, stop my clothes from moulding in the damp. I walked the miles of beach on the weekends, in whipping wind, crushed the heads of kelp with my soft boots.

Chinlac

Morning we go in to Chinlac it pours, doesn't let up till we start at 11:00 a.m. and the muddy road to the trail is flanked by excavators, fallers, trailers for the loggers to fill up on coffee.

Peter in the back seat with his white-haired dog, Phoebe, built the trail in years ago. Fit and sixty-one, still a beaming Boy Scout passionate about beauty the earth shows. He wants to reveal it, clear away tangled brush and muddled minds. Hatchet sticking out of his canvas backpack is for hacking the small stuff; there has been a lot of blowdown in the past few blustery months. Though it is summer, sun has yet to warm the earth and water floats on top of the soggy soil, waiting to sink in. Janice and I are in recovery from a late night with wine at the campfire, when she decided to join me.

"Take two ibuprofen and drink a ton of water before bed and I'll tap on your window in the morning," I told her. And it worked, minimal headache, though the scratching of a pack rat skimmed the edge of sleep. Thought it was under the bed, but it was beneath the floor of the cabin, trying to find a way in.

Sign for the provincial parking lot, brown with white carved letters, is pounded to a pine tree. Parking lot is mush. When I pull in, Peter says I should turn the car around; if anything happens we want to be sure we can get out fast. He is matter-of-fact, pointing out survival strategies natural to a forester. He gathers his maps, shows me the squiggly trail. I stare at it blankly, anxious to get going. It's a two-hour hike under the best of conditions, which we do not have. So he rolls them up, leaves them in the back. Later, I will look at them and wonder what squiggly lines we actually did trace through the bush.

"I forgot my lunch!" he cries out.

"That's okay. We've got bologna sandwiches, some cantaloupe..." says Janice. A lab tech, mother of three, practical, enthusiastic, she is prepared. She even brought foam bug dope you can spread on your face, the back of your hands. Before we start, Peter combs his perfectly cut white hair and pulls on a Norwegian knit toque. He shows us his sensible wool pants, orange rain coveralls, mirrored compass. I am in jeans, rain gear and ankle-length hiking boots; Janice in running shoes, Cleveland Indians ball cap perched on her head. We are completely soaked within the first five minutes, edging around deep mud pools that inhabit the path. Bush is lush, much more than last summer when the dry heat scorched the green to a mottled brown. Looked like disease but it was just thirst.

Dene

Chief Khadintel was not at the village when the Chilcotin arrived on the shores of the lake. He had left early in the morning before the village had woken to inspect snares further up the Nechako River. He liked the stillness of the dawn, the sound of his footsteps soft on the earth. Violent marauders did not wait for him to return; they annihilated the village with vengeance. Hatchets and arrows flying, panicked thud of feet, hands and knees pummelling the earth. Terrified, a few young men ran away to the surrounding forest, in search of their chief. They came across him on the banks of the river and Khadintel could tell by their stricken faces that the Chilcotin had come and he knew they had come for him.

"I am the one they want, you must run back to the forest to save your lives. I alone ought to die."

Chinlac

Through the thin stands sprouts of new trees cover the earth and a full-throated creek rushes clear and cold. "We used to portage a seventy-pound canoe down this path," Peter tells us. First part of the trail is a road that meets and then follows the swollen Nechako, leading to a switchback up a ridge to an esker, he tells us.

"Do you know what an esker is?" he calls over his shoulder. Dollar-size leaves flip silver sides in the breeze. Rain cloud hovers; I hope it will hold. I don't know what an esker is but it is a beautiful word, like a baby Eskimo.

He doesn't wait for a response. He is spouting knowledge, unstoppable, "An esker is a long, winding ridge of sand and stratified gravel, mainly found in glaciated and formerly glaciated areas of Europe and North America. Eskers are often several kilometres long and have a peculiar uniform shape."

Phoebe trots ahead, follows scents off the trail but always comes back. She is silent, steady. I am always relieved to have dogs around, a kind of sonar for what lies ahead, though some say they bring back bears. When we reach the Nechako, pink and yellow ribbons are tied to trunks. Pinks are Peter's and yellows are from a friend with a GPS, I gather from his conversation, mainly with Janice.

"I've been doing this for years, ladies, and I know the best way in and out. Not always the fastest. GPS'll tell you to cut clear through," he explains but I barely follow through the exertion of trying not to slip in the pools that widen as we walk.

We stop on a ridge and the river, twice its normal size, is languid, braiding ribbons bubbling brown sugar. Across from us is an abandoned ferry dock, white platform still half in the water, half on shore. Ferry brought miners and foresters to work and it cut down on building bridges—not that there ever was one. Grass on the landing is long and leaning from the weight of water. I want to stay longer but the mosquitoes descend in a merciless haze. Janice and I move towards the trail but Peter stands behind us, a half-dozen mosquitoes feasting on his face. He wipes them away in a bloody swipe.

"What are foresters like?" I ask. Peter has been building trails, planning logging roads for years, mainly on his own. "Foresters are individuals. Independent. Bit on the extreme. On both ends, I'd say. We like people. We don't like people." He smiles at me, gentle misanthrope. When I asked him to take us, he was reluctant but then he relented. "If it's important to you, I will take you," he said, like he needed some time to gather himself, not for the bush, but for us.

DENE

Khadintel could see the canoes of the avenging warriors rounding the curve of the river, slowing at the sight of him, sudden war cries coming from the dark of their open mouths. Terrified, the young men scrambled up the bank but the chief stayed to face his enemy, his feet and body doing a crazy dance, nimbly dodging all the arrows whizzing by. Khalpan, the captain of the war party, stopped the attack. He didn't want to waste more arrows. What if the Chinlac chief was charmed, watched over by strong spirits?

"Khadintel, you have the reputation of being a man and I see you are a good dancer. You have danced for your life once. If you are a man, dance for me again."

CHINLAC

Submerged trail means we have to bushwhack to get to the steep ridge on our left. And we plough through, Peter leading the way. Undergrowth is light, you can see ahead but it hides slippery trees you can fit your hands around, black from rot but still solid obstacles. We huff up and down, following what becomes a kind of slough beside us, accompanied by a trill that declares *I am here*. "What's that bird?" I ask Janice and Peter at a brief stop. Slough around the esker is rounding a bend and it looks like we'll have to backtrack to where we started to reach the ridge.

"Don't know my birds, just the bush," Peter says. Off the trail we see things. Half-eaten deer announced by smell of decay, ripped in half by a hungry bear. Curve of jaw and hollow eye socket, rounded ribs in one spot, bent legs with bits of hide clinging in another.

"Sounds like a chickadee," Janice says.

"I read somewhere that chickadees only sing in isolation," I say. I've seen pictures; they are full-breasted, black-capped, aware.

"Something has been sleeping here," Peter points to a round space crushed by weight.

"Bear sleeping close to the food?" I say. A pause and no one answers. Raw death sleep satiated hunger.

"I've lived here for twenty-five years and this is the

first time I've bushwhacked!" Janice breaks the silence. Sweating, smiling face, rosy cheeked, straight brown bangs plastered to her wide forehead. Wanted to climb Fraser Mountain, but any adventure would do, she told me, throw herself unplanned into the thick, see what comes out. Peter is her neighbour, she waves at him when she goes jogging but he doesn't remember her. All of us have fallen, lurching off slippery wood into prickly bushes, getting back up, wetter, muddier. Forty minutes of backtracking and finally the steep side of the ridge rises like a green wall.

"At least you can see what's up ahead here. In Haida Gwaii, salal was so massive you didn't know the direction you were going when you came out," I say. We have all wanted to turn back at some point, but not at the same time. "My instinct was to head for the ridge, skip all this," Peter said, surveying the swamp we had slogged around and through. I had wanted to follow the path, so I could come back another time, know my way, but water had forced us to improvise.

Peter showed us his scar, jagged red indent on his right forearm like the sharp curve of the trail we were taking. "Nearly lost my arm, chainsaw skidded off a log and cut to the bone. I was by myself, half-hour from the road." Though we're up out of the muck, the ridge isn't as dry as it looks, I keep slipping. "So I hold my arm up, tie a rag at the elbow. Blood is running down my arm, my side, filling up my boots. I want to lie down, feel light-headed, but I keep moving. Phoebe was with me."

DENE

To show that he was in control of his emotions, that the fear and pain of death could not overcome him, the chief danced on the beach of the river, but this time a traditional dance of the Carrier people, slow and rhythmic his feet touched the earth and he sang in a cracked voice. He was sure he was going to die and he thought how he was not prepared, that he was a selfish man. The warriors watched and jeered at him, trying to break his spirit, but as he continued to dance it came to him that if he survived, his job was to gather the bones of the dead and heal the earth as best he could.

"You are a strong man," Khalpan said. He stood in the canoe, his arms across his chest. "We will leave you with your life."

CHINLAC

ATV tracks suddenly emerge and we cheer, trudging turns to walking and we start to look around. Bloated brown Nechako just to the right of the Slough of Despond now below us.

"I got to the truck keeping my arm up, and I called the ambulance when I got close enough, using the radio phone. Told them get here quick or I'm going to die. I got in and drove straight, that's why I told you to turn around. Never know what's going to happen."

Above the tree line and still no birds. Esker is the next winding stage, slippery, like walking on the back of a snake. Peter says it's about two thirds of the way there. Four different environments take us to the site, he tells us. First, boreal forest along the creek, then the meadow by the river, then the eskers and finally Chinlac, which is on a level plain thirty feet above the Stuart.

"Ambulance met me on the way to Fraser Lake. By then my boots were full of blood and I tried to tourniquet my arm. Lucky I didn't or I would've lost it. We sped to emergency and the attendants were so quiet, I think I was yelling at them. The doctor, I still remember his face, he was tired, you know? And he looked at me like *Oh my God* but he saved my life." Halted suddenly by gratitude, he stops and looks over his shoulder at us, blue boyish eyes. Sun starting to warm the edges of the day, we shuck a layer of coats, rain pants. Air some skin. Lean over trail edges around a sheer drop. River fills the whole frame, smudged green reflects on the brown. Peter takes our picture but it doesn't turn out; we are blocked by light, just an outline of bulk and smiles.

He tells us that we are walking through a burn that looks recent, trunks tarred up to the edge of our ribs. But it was four years ago. Earth has not recovered. Spindly growth doesn't absorb our voices; they fly like arrows in the silence.

"Notice anything different?" Peter quizzes.

Janice sees it right away. "The burn stops at the edge!"

"Yes! The burn stops at the edge, and that's where the trail is, where it always has been. Carrier feet made the original trail that we're walking on." Burn is the natural border then as it is now. We are finally on the path and it feels like hauling onto shore after a long swim. Peter says something like you can still see footprints if you brush away leaves and topsoil, careful excavation revealing scuffs of toes and heels. Raw years marked with fire, tough feet holding to the edge.

DENE

As the Chilcotin departed, Khadintel, shaking badly, forced himself to stand straight as he could. Even so, his shoulders sagged like an old cow. But he howled his vengeance, that one day he would come like a nightmare to their village and avenge their marauding and the Chilcotin again jeered and laughed at him. The young men came silent as ghosts out of the forest and they all returned to the village. Everywhere there were broken bodies and the earth was bathed in blood. There were two long, sturdy poles planted in the ground and on thick forked sticks the bodies of children hung, ripped open and spitted through turned out ribs like drying salmon.

CHINLAC

Fork in the road down a steep hill gives us pause. Yellow and pink ribbons separate, go their own way. I am really starving now. "How long till we get there?" I am plaintive.

"Thirty minutes from here if we take the pink line across the burn. Heard the yellow line is full of blowdown, it'll slow us down. Though it's by the river, way prettier." He shows us the confluence of the sleepy skein of the Nechako slipping into the muscling Stuart; two rivers, negotiating curves and obstacles at their own speed, converging in a circling maelstrom.

"Why do they move so differently? A river's a river, right?" I ask. No one answers. We all turn left to cut across; fastest is best this time. "This trail was done by GPS, should take us pretty close to the site. It's not what I built, what I made took time, I considered the beauty, what was easier going in, coming out." Peter's voice is indignant, that the best way has been so quickly sidetracked by a machine. His Boy Scout energy is unflagging as ours starts to, out of hunger, weariness.

Land flattens, desert plain offering brief oasis. Death pulls stronger than life here, surrender to enormous force. Undertow of silence sharpens thin blades of grass tufting, clumps of scraggly growth. Earth listless, hasn't recovered. Bright pink ribbon flashes in the blackened grey stalks, leafless branches. Sky brings heat on a frigid wave, season seems confused. Beneath us, dirt hardened by thousands of footsteps.

"See these holes?" Peter points out deep indents, about two feet down and around, packed close together, pockmarks on the level ground. There are twenty-two hundred of them, he tells us. "People from Chinlac smoked their food and buried it here. Generations used the same spot." We are cutting through, so we'll miss most of them, he says. If we circled the perimeter, we would lose our breath counting.

DENE

Khadintel surrendered to his fate, he burned all the bodies and saved the bones, placing them in leather satchels for the surviving relatives of the victims. For three years he sang and prayed and danced on the earth of the village, trying to bring it back to life. But his heart was full of pain and rage at his loss and he could not rest until the massacre was avenged. In the spring of the third year, he prepared to journey to Khalpan's village with a war party built from allied bands in the area, from Stoney Creek, from Natleh. They travelled deep into Chilcotin territory and passed the night in a terrace above the long row of lodges where the Chilcotin lived. Though his men slept well in the dark, Khadintel lay awake and watched the stars of the night shift above him, knowing that if he slept he would have the nightmare of despair, of torn flesh and howling dogs that had tormented him for three years. The next day the Carrier soldiers moved stealthily through the forest to attack.

CHINLAC

Final pink ribbon takes us to the edge of the swirling Stuart. Dead grass, blackened rotting trunks circle around us. Opposite bank is high and green, looks healthy in comparison. "Where do we go from here?" I ask. Rush of river is welcome after eerie hush.

"Chinlac is downriver ten minutes or so," Peter is already scrambling over a log; bedraggled, we follow. All I can think about is food. Should have eaten more this morning but all I could handle was coffee and a bun. Silence spreads over us from the clearing in a mute wave. A hollow space, a vacuum the size of a baseball field. Knee-high grass. Yellow heads of wild daisies. At the centre a skeleton teepee stands, desiccated sage hanging from a string. Heading towards it, our feet feel out the edges of ghost buildings.

"Thirteen houses were built here along the edge of the bank," Peter calls out.

"I thought the Carrier were nomadic," I say.

"They were and they weren't. I don't know. Maybe after the massacre no one wanted to live here anymore, they became nomadic."

"What's with the outhouse?" Janice says. Dark green, modern, it looks odd, plopped down.

"It's for Carrier ceremonies. There're some white boards in the bush, they make them into bleachers."

Chinlac was a thriving community for a thousand years before the massacre. A Ming dynasty coin was found in the dirt. Arrow tips, tools, made by knowing hands. No digging happens now; the Carrier won't allow it. Enough has been uncovered and the land has gone back to sleep. Finally, we settle on the banks and Janice unpacks lunch, squished sandwiches, crushed cantaloupe. We are ravenous.

"Many people who come here say this is a sacred place," Peter says. I've heard this before—how people are moved by it, like you are in a temple or a church, some kind of holy place. Across the river tall dead trees' gnarled branches wave at us.

"Why aren't there any nests there?" Janice says. We sit eating in restful silence. Wind blows wisps of grass between us.

Peter talks about how the Carrier kids in town should help him make a better trail instead of playing video games, watching TV. This is their heritage, after all. He tells us that in his yard he has cut huge swathes of branches from a beautiful spruce near the top and the bottom in the Carrier way, so he can see what's coming the way they did. Dried grey wood carried by the river collects at the tip of a narrow island just below us.

DENE

Khalpan was not in the village that day, but his younger brother, 'Kun'qus, heard the marauders approaching as he was checking salmon traps and rushed back to the village. Kind, stubborn, strong, thick legs, round belly, his footsteps thundered on the earth. Rumours that had spread through the Chinlac village before its own demise had then spread through the Chilcotin village. 'Kun'qus was wise and fortified his house. His first wife plastered the walls, watched over his adored son, but his second slave Carrier wife was sullen, threw stones and sticks at him. 'Kun'qus did not sleep well the night before, feeling an uneasy sense of eyes watching from the forest, silent and cunning. As he approached his home, passing his Carrier wife crying and running to her people, he ran after her with his war club in hand, but he gave up and returned to the fight and to protect his first wife and young son.

Chinlac

Peter gets up to look for another trail out besides the one we took. He has been here many times and talks through the silence, so I'm grateful for the moment of quiet, a full stomach. Think about the eyes that watched the bank I'm looking at, watched the wood gather, the ones who named this place Chinlac.

"So. Was it worth it?" I ask Janice. We share a chocolate bar, melted a bit but still crunchy. "Absolutely! It's beautiful but so quiet. Weird quiet."

"I know. No birds."

"And no birds sang," she adds, like it is the name of a song, or book.

I get up to walk around, get a feel of the weight. Try to discern the pull. Trees only grow so close to the clearing, then stop. My feet feel out the edges of things, shapes of places that still take up space. When Peter was talking I thought I heard singing, a hearty male voice, but there was nothing when I paced the place. Maybe voices weave in when we're not really listening, subtle like grass binding with flowers.

Peter is back, talking to Janice when I return, triumphant with a rusted tin can in his hand. "I found a midden! Which is a nice word for garbage pile. This must have been Borden's stash. Probably a can of milk, you can see the punctures." Charles Borden was the archeologist who excavated the site in the fifties, wrote a book, got famous. His book is lying on my living room floor, full of graphs and lists and maps.

"Follow me. I'll show you where we come in by canoe," Peter calls over his shoulder. We come across a stone just before the steep climb down to the water. A story is spelled out in Carrier shapes and symbols, round loops and straight backs. We stare at it dumbly. "English is on the other side!" Janice calls out.

"Here it says that the massacre was over women," she says.

"I thought they had killed a chief," I add. Stone says Chun-lac. "And it's not Chinlac. We've been saying it wrong."

DENE

'Kun'qus' wife sobbed as she helped him into his wooden warrior armour, the sleeveless moose-skin tunic slathered with glue and gravel. Fighting back tears he watched his people fall, shooting arrow after arrow, he squeezed his son between his legs but an arrow struck the young boy in the heart. 'Kun'qus fought the urge to lie down with his dead son, let the earth take them both. Carrier warriors set upon him like hungry dogs, but he held them off with a stone dagger, slicing the air. Then one Carrier warrior dodged his lance and held it, and the avengers swarmed him, clubbed him between the eyes, bludgeoned his body. Dead children were butchered and splayed on three poles instead of two and then the marauders left the village.

CHINLAC

It's too steep and we're too tired to go down to the river. Launch area is submerged but Peter points it out anyway, it will emerge when the water stops swallowing. Coming by canoe is the ancient way, how it was done for hundreds of years. We would see Chinlac the way the Carrier did, the way their friends and enemies did, by climbing up the bank.

"That's what the Chilcotin did," I say. "Paddled in quietly, got out with their bows, arrows, spears. Probably smeared paint on their faces, braced themselves for war. Just women and children were here, the men had gone fishing." I stand on the edge, trying to imagine fierce warriors coming up the bank. Silence of shock, then running, screaming, some young men escaping the slaughter, trying to find their chief, Khadintel, whose misdeed was being avenged with such brutal force. Try to imagine Khadintel's face changing as he sees them coming, alarm spreading through their lean limbs and into the ground.

Janice tells us it's four and we should be heading back. Sun has relaxed, spread out across the whole sky. And we walk to where the emptiness meets the trees, from the in-between into the world again. There is no singing, bold voice swallowed up or stubbornly silent. We clamber over the same trees to get to the first pink ribbon. Peter points across a sand bar in the middle of the river. "That's where Khadintel, the Carrier chief, danced for his life." See him dancing and crying, dancing and crying, the Chilcotin chief taunting him. But were the men quiet or jeering who watched safe in the canoes? I can't hear them. They had just flayed flesh, torched dried hides, dragged off young women to be their slaves, killed the old ones. Long history. Sudden stop.

DENE

Returning from his fishing trip, Khalpan sensed an unnatural silence as he approached the village that turned him cold, but then panicked yelps and howls of dogs crying for their masters broke through the air. Carrier had come, hunting for him. Smell of smoke-singed hair hovered above the clearing of the village, splashed with carnage and blood. Brother half swallowed by the earth, family dead, ripped arms and torsos strewn by vengeful storm. Lonely daughter taken as a slave. Greatly shaken, he set out with the other survivors to pursue the Carrier. No stealth in his shaking legs, feet dragging, clumsy. At a fork in the river the warriors were preparing to leave. They all stopped to stare at the chief, hollow-eyed, but it was Khadintel who stepped forward to meet him.

"They say that you are a man, and you call yourself a terrible warrior," Khadintel said in Chilcotin. "If you are, come to meet me and do not retreat."

CHINLAC

Way back is always shorter than the way in. Body eases up and down, jagged corners become gentle curves. Sun helps, brightens things.

"The massacre happened in seventeen forty-five. After all the buildings and bodies were burned, the village was abandoned," I tell Janice. Peter is up ahead, he has told us all of his concerns and is quiet on the way back.

"It's strange that it is so empty," I say. "After all that time, something should have grown there. Nature always takes over."

"Nothing will ever grow there," she says, like she is sure. Passionate gardener, she knows more about growing things than I do.

We stay on the high ridge back, edge around the Slough of Despond. I have given up on following the trail—I know it is waiting to be revealed when the water goes. And I trust Peter, he is gallant, apologizing for taking us through ATV tracks, deer trails and Carrier footsteps until he decides to check his compass, make sure we hit the wide trail near the Nechako.

"Do you know what a culturally modified tree is?" Peter asks. We have stopped by a spruce with a broken branch. Mosquitoes dive to our exposed skin.

"I don't know!" I cry out.

"Yeah, the mosquitoes are bad," he takes another bloody swipe at his face. "Anything that has been changed by people. See this branch? It was broken on purpose to mark a direction in the trail. Carriers did it all the time."

"Like trees become part of the path," I say, wanting to be a good pupil, but Peter has charged ahead. "What hasn't been changed by people," I tell Janice. Probably every step we are taking has been taken before. No part of here is untouched.

Khalpan moved on shaky legs, strength seeping out, gush of blood thundering his temples. Enemy stood still, flexed, glaring and he could not face them, inched back to the forest, crying.

"Now, Khalpan," Khadintel, triumphant, bellowed, "when, all alone against your people, I was cornered on the riverbank and you wanted to kill me, I danced for you. If you are a man, dance now for me, as I did for you."

CHINLAC

When we finally make it back to my car Peter has declared our trip the worst ever in all his years. Day is marked by dubious honour.

"You were troopers, stellar, I tell you," he says and we laugh, relieved to be sitting, safe from the bugs. Phoebe is huddled on her blanket, her white hairs are floating with the dust in the waning light. It's six-thirty, two and a half hours back but it felt faster, like we were helped or hurried along. Heading back to the highway, lemon fields of alfalfa wave to us. At Peter's house, he shows us the tree we can see through, cars speeding around a curve below. Canoes and kayaks in his garage.

"Don't have a car. I walk or ride my bike everywhere, so Phoebe can come with me." Smiles his boyish grin, goes into the dark of his house.

DENE

Khalpan stood on the beach and remembered all his relatives and friends gone and his daughter dragged into slavery. "Please spare my daughter's life!" he howled. Wracking grief, retching, he fell to his hands and knees. Silent Carrier watched, no birds flew or sang overhead. Sobbing, Khalpan hauled himself up, faced his enemy.

Khadintel, scornful, jeered: "Khalpan, we sought revenge upon the men of your village to repair the great wrong you set on us, but you weep like a woman, so I will let you live. Go in peace, and weep to your heart's content."

CHINLAC

Around the campfire at Fraser Lake, my feet drying
on hot stones, I roll out the maps. One of them is by
Father Morice, famous oblate of Fort St. James who
spoke Carrier, Chilcotin, wrote the story of the Chin-
lac massacre. Map is dated 1907. Dot of Fort George.
In random spots, words written: *light soil, natural prairies,
undulating with small meadows.* Janice and I hunch over,
hot dogs in hand, we find Chinlac written in fine hand,
just down from *wavy rapids,* on the *swift and shallow* Stu-
art River. Indian trails traced in perforated lines. Sun
sets, map squiggles start to fade but I find a little horse-
shoe above Summit Lake, where he wrote *Stuart River
springs from here from the ground about knee wide.* I roll it
up, watch the flames descend to cinders, cold nipping at
my back. Walk weary to bed.

Mosquito Lake

Lucy dreams killer whales with shark teeth slice the lake. For three nights now naked fish deer children fight for shore. She sees Nigel, hears him calling, waving his arms, arrows strewn around his wounded waist. In his eyes pained, deep offering. When the lake dries up, starts to burn, she wakes Toby. *Let's get out of here.* Drums beat the fist of invasion. The engine struggles, wheels roll, mountain heaves. Screeching birds claw at the space between her eyes, where the nightmare peaks. Killer whale turns reptile, talons tear the earth. What she dreamed before was shadows on grass, effortless flight. They sleep on an abandoned logging road, crossed by fallen trees. She wakes up, rolls over, drags souls like sacks of sand to the shore. The dream won't leave the lake.

ACKNOWLEDGEMENTS

Thank you to my family for their faith in me and for always being there to come home to. Christophe and Leanne Lengagne, I am so grateful for your enduring friendship. I have wonderful friends who have encouraged and cajoled me through all my mishaps but never discouraged my spirit of adventure.

I am grateful for the stories of the Carrier and Chilcotin, which have given me a deeper knowledge of the land I grew up in.

Thank you to my inspiring cohorts at UNBC and Prince George—great writers and artists. Such fun.

Special thanks for the guidance and encouragement I received from Al Rempel, Rob Budde and Kristen Guest.

Most of all, thanks to the people I had the honour to travel with: Katrina Hoelting, Shannon Day-Cheung, Janice Gairdner, Sarah Colgrove, Kelly Posthuma, Winnie Lam and Peter Rodseth. Thank you for letting me share your experiences.

Casey, Edward S. *Getting Back into Place: Toward a Renewed Understanding of the Place-world.* Bloominton: University of Indiana Press. 1993.

___.*Remembering:A Phenomenological Study.* Bloomington: University of Indiana Press. 1987.

Cresswell, Tim. *Place: A Short Introduction.* Oxford: Blackwell Publishing. 2004.

Foote, Kenneth. E. *Shadowed Ground: America's landscape of Violence and Tragedy.* Austin: University of Texas Press. 1997.

Hessler, Peter. *River Town: Two Years of the Yangtze.* London: John Murray Publishers. 2001.

Leighly, John. ed. *Land and Life: A Selection of Writings of Carl Ortwin Sauer.* Berkeley: University of California Press. 1963.

___."The Morphology of Landscape." 315- 350.

Malpas, J.E. *Place and Experience: A Philosophical Topography.* Cambridge: Cambridge University Press. 1999.

Morice, A.G. *The History of the Northern Interior of British Columbia.* Smithers : Interior Stationary. 1970.
Schama, Simon. *Landscape and Memory.* New York: Alfred A. Knopf. 1995.

Smith, Mick. Laura Cameron, Joyce Davidson, Liz Bondi.eds.*Emotion,Place and Culture.*Aldershot:Ashgate. 2009.

Hua, Anh. *"What we all long for: Memory, Trauma and Emotional Geographies."* 135-148.

Tuan, Yi-Fu. Topophilia: *A Study of Environmental Perception, Attitudes, and Values.* New York: Columbia University Press. 1974.

Photo Josh Massey

Adrienne Fitzpatrick earned her master's in English at the University of Northern British Columbia, where she completed a creative thesis. Her fiction, poetry and creative non-fiction have appeared in *Prairie Fire*, *CV2* and *subTerrain*, and she is one of the poetry editors for *Room* magazine. *The Earth Remembers Everything* is her first book.